MAXnotes®

D0920564

Joseph Conrad's

Heart of Darkness

Text by
Frank Fiorenza
(M.A., The College of Staten Island)
Department of English
Moore High School
Staten Island, New York

Illustrations by
Thomas E. Cantillon

Research & Education Association
Dr. M. Fogiel, Director

MAXnotes® for
HEART OF DARKNESS

Printed in the United States of America

Library of Congress Control Number 00-191839

International Standard Book Number 0-87891-017-4

MAXnotes® is a registered trademark of
Research & Education Association, Piscataway, New Jersey 08854

What **MAXnotes**® *Will Do for You*

This book is intended to help you absorb the essential contents and features of Joseph Conrad's *Heart of Darkness* and to help you gain a thorough understanding of the work. Our book has been designed to do this more quickly and effectively than any other study guide.

For best results, this **MAXnotes** book should be used as a companion to the actual work, not instead of it. The interaction between the two will greatly benefit you.

To help you in your studies, this book presents the most up-to-date interpretations of every section of the actual work, followed by questions and fully explained answers that will enable you to analyze the material critically. The questions also will help you to test your understanding of the work and will prepare you for discussions and exams.

Meaningful illustrations are included to further enhance your understanding and enjoyment of the literary work. The illustrations are designed to place you into the mood and spirit of the work's settings.

The **MAXnotes** also include summaries, character lists, explanations of plot, and section-by-section analyses. A biography of the author and discussion of the work's historical context will help you put this literary piece into the proper framework of what is taking place.

The use of this study guide will save you the hours of preparation time that would ordinarily be required to arrive at a complete grasp of this work of literature. You will be well-prepared for classroom discussions, homework, and exams. The guidelines that are included for writing papers and reports on various topics will prepare you for any added work which may be assigned.

The **MAXnotes** will take your grades "to the max."

Dr. Max Fogiel
Program Director

Contents

Section One: *Introduction* 1

The Life and Work of Joseph Conrad 1

Historical Background 4

Master List of Characters 7

Summary of the Novel 8

Estimated Reading Time 11

> **Each section includes List of Characters, Summary, Analysis, Study Questions and Answers, and Suggested Essay Topics.**

Section Two: *Heart of Darkness* 12

Section I 12

Section Three: *Heart of Darkness* 34

Section II 34

Section Four: *Heart of Darkness* 54

Section III 54

Section Five: *Sample Analytical Paper Topics* 77

Section Six: *Bibliography* 84

MAXnotes® are simply the best – but don't just take our word for it...

"... I have told every bookstore in the area to carry your MAXnotes. They are the only notes I recommend to my students. There is no comparison between MAXnotes and all other notes ..."
 – *High School Teacher & Reading Specialist,*
 Arlington High School, Arlington, MA

"... I discovered the MAXnotes when a friend loaned me her copy of the *MAXnotes for Romeo and Juliet.* The book really helped me understand the story. Please send me a list of stores in my area that carry the MAXnotes. I would like to use more of them ..."
 – *Student, San Marino, CA*

"... The two MAXnotes titles that I have used have been very, very useful in helping me understand the subject matter reviewed. Thank you for creating the MAXnotes series ..."
 – *Student, Morrisville, PA*

A Glance at Some of the Characters

Charlie Marlow

The Manager

Two Knitting Women

The Helmsman

The Russian

Kurtz

Kurtz's Intended

Kurtz's Mistress

SECTION ONE

Introduction

The Life and Work of Joseph Conrad

In a part of Russia that once belonged to Poland, Joseph Conrad was born Josef Teodor Konrad Nalecz Korzeniowski on December 3, 1857, to his parents, Apollo and Evelina. Members of the landed gentry, his parents believed in liberating Poland, though from opposite extremes. Apollo Korzeniowski came from a family dedicated to the romantic idealism of their cause, eager to act, if necessary, to die for Poland. Though championing the same beliefs, Evelina Bobrowski's family advocated working quietly for their goal, and surviving as best they could under the dictates of the occupying power. Their concerns deeply influenced Conrad's upbringing.

Apollo devoted his life to literary interests and political involvement. He wrote plays and poems of little value, but adeptly translated Victor Hugo and Shakespeare into Polish. In 1862, Conrad's father started a literary journal, *Fortnightly Review*. Politically, Apollo's main concern centered around fortifying resistance against Russian oppression. He helped organize the National Central Committee. He joined a radical wing and was arrested before he took any action. Exiled to the Vologda region of northern Russia in 1862, Apollo longed to have his family accompany him.

Already physically fragile, Conrad's mother suffered under the harshness of exile. The strain of imprisonment hastened her death in 1865 at thirty-four, less than three years after their exile. Authorities allowed Apollo to move to southern Russia after his wife's death. Suffering from tuberculosis later in life, and not considered a threat anymore, Apollo returned home. He spent his last months in Cracow, where he died in 1869.

By the time Conrad was a teenager, he had suffered from his family's political involvement. At four, he saw his father arrested; at seven, he saw his mother die; and, at eleven, he saw his father die. He was left in the care of his uncle, Thaddeus Bobrowski. These traumatic experiences stayed with Conrad for his entire life. They fueled his wish to flee Poland. Consequently, they also instilled in him feelings of desertion, betrayal, and guilt for leaving his homeland. These themes were explored deeply in his work, *Lord Jim*.

From his parents' tribulations, Conrad concluded that no future lay in store for him in Poland. He needed to escape to fashion a life based on his inner promptings. His desire to see other countries led him to say as he looked at a map of Africa, "When I grow up I shall go there." That place was the Belgian Congo, which became the germ for *Heart of Darkness*.

By traveling, Conrad could secure economic independence, live out adventures, and escape political unrest. Since his uncle had connections in the shipping industry and French was his second language, the French merchant marine attracted him, even though he had never seen the sea. The excitement he had read about in the works of Victor Hugo and James Fenimore Cooper could now become part of his life. His Polish relatives viewed his choice of becoming a sailor as an insult to his cultural background.

Two months before his seventeenth birthday, in 1874, Conrad left for Marseilles and a sea career. The four years he spent on French ships gave him the richness of experience he longed for. He sailed to the West Indies, and Central and South America. On his second voyage, he met Spanish rebels and smuggled guns on their behalf. With his ship wrecked on the Spanish coast, Conrad escaped to France. He fictionalized these experiences in his novels *Nostromo* (1904) and *The Arrow of Gold* (1919).

At this time he met Dona Rita, a Spanish rebel. He supposedly fought a pistol duel with an American, Captain Blunt, over her. Both were wounded. Rita and Blunt disappeared by the time Thaddeus arrived. Conrad told his uncle he had lost money gambling and had tried to commit suicide, he said nothing about the duel. Here, his adventures in France ended.

After turning twenty, Conrad switched allegiances to Britain by becoming an English seaman. He did so for two reasons: he wanted to flee the obligation to the Russian military forces and he thought that if he learned English, he could be promoted sooner.

Modern British literature profited from Conrad's defection from the French seas. There is a good possibility he would not have undertaken his writing career in English if he had not joined the British navy. In 1886, the same year he was naturalized as a British citizen, Conrad passed his examinations for master mariner. By then it was clear his life had settled and he had made a wise choice.

Conrad served on British ships for nearly twelve years. As second mate, he sailed on a ship journeying between Singapore and Borneo. He sailed to the Orient on the *Palestine,* a ship that burned and sank off the coast of Java. He used this adventure in *Youth* (1902). In 1888, ten years after his switch from the French to British seas, he commanded his only ship, the *Otago.* His novella, *The Secret Sharer,* reflects this experience. His one interlude from the British service was when he piloted a river boat to the Belgian Congo, the basis for *Heart of Darkness.* This journey also affected his health, a consequence which may have influenced his switch from seaman to writer.

He began writing his first novel, *Almayer's Folly,* in 1889, though he did not in any way consider himself a writer. He eventually submitted the manuscript in 1894; it was accepted after Edward Garnett read it. Through Garnett's encouragement, Conrad began writing another novel. He still pursued a sea career, however, attempting to secure a command until 1898. For the next thirteen years, he wrote nearly one volume per year.

Married and with two sons, Conrad found it difficult to live off his literary earnings, even though he lived modestly in country homes. He received a Civil List pension from the British government.

After twenty years and sixteen volumes, Conrad finally achieved popular success with his novel *Chance* (1913). His limited audience grew to a wider acceptance.

During his literary career, Conrad met and made friends with Stephen Crane, H. G. Wells, Ford Madox Ford, and Henry James—influential writers of their time. Even with their friendships, he lived outside the mainstream of literary life. He was unaware of Freud's work and other scientific advances. He knew nothing of James

Joyce, Virginia Woolf, and D. H. Lawrence—writers with whom his work is often compared. Yet, his relative isolation did not prevent him from formulating his philosophy about art, fiction, and their relation to life. Many of the prefaces of his novels serve as his foundation for his artistic beliefs.

Often linked to Herman Melville and Jack London, other writers of adventure stories, Conrad infused his work with psychological and moral implications. His characters face deep problems, ones with difficult or no answers. Their response to these questions often determines the course of their lives. Symbol and myth fill his fiction, and much of his story lies beneath the surface narrative. The adventure is merely one level of the story, the more intriguing one is buried under the plot. Reading a work by Conrad requires patience, diligence, and concentration.

From his first book, he used "Joseph Conrad" as his writing name, his difficult given name had been misspelled too many times on official sailing papers. A master craftsman and stylist, Conrad labored at the writing process. No writing came easy to him. His major works include *Almayer's Folly* (1895), *The Nigger of the Narcissus* (1897), *Lord Jim* (1900), *Youth*—containing *Heart of Darkness* (1902), *Nostromo* (1904), *The Secret Agent* (1907), *The Secret Sharer* (1910), *Under Western Eyes* (1911), and *Victory* (1915).

Never a healthy man, Conrad suffered from indigestion, hypochondria, and melancholia. Conrad died at his desk in 1924, at the age of sixty-six. A man who did not speak English before he was twenty-two, and did not write English until he taught himself at thirty-two, Joseph Conrad fashioned his life at sea into his life in fiction. By transforming experience into art, he established his permanence as a twentieth-century British novelist.

Historical Background

Conrad based *Heart of Darkness* on his journey to the Belgian Congo in 1890. By checking his diaries at the time, we can trace his experience against his fictional portrayal. But this novella is more than an autobiographical account of his time spent there. It is a modern work that challenges the basic ethical question of good and evil in mankind, a topic explored by many authors. We need only think of the Adam and Eve myth, Milton's *Paradise Lost*,

Dante's *Divine Comedy*, Golding's *Lord of the Flies*, and Burgess's *A Clockwork Orange* to name a few. Francis Ford Coppola based his film, *Apocalypse Now*, on this philosophical concept by updating Conrad's story to the Vietnam War and the Southeast Asian jungle of the 1960s.

Conrad also tackled the political environment of the Congo in *Heart of Darkness*. When King Leopold of Belgium founded the "International Association for the Suppression of Slavery and the Opening Up of Central Africa," he attempted to impose civilization and order. Greed, though, fostered widespread abuse. By the time Conrad visited the Congo, exploitation festered everywhere. Brutality and degradation reigned, not progress and enlightenment. The natives' sufferings and Kurtz's writings about them reflect the historical reality.

A number of factors influenced Conrad and other twentieth-century British writers. We have to first understand Victorian England and the reasons why the modern novelist rejected the values and beliefs of that time to mold a new society founded on different ideals.

Victorian England believed in materialism and progress. Their bourgeois (middle class) values served to stabilize all facets of society, so they believed. The writings of Jane Austen, Charles Dickens and George Eliot represented the standards of their time, with *Pride and Prejudice*, *Great Expectations*, and *Middlemarch* serving as landmarks in fiction at that time. Their novels usually followed the traditional three-volume format. They focussed on many details, often writing at length about seemingly insignificant details.

As the era closed, reaction against Victorian life, commercialism, and community spread. The artist stood, not as a member of society, but in isolation from it. Once embraced by authors, religious faith even declined.

With formal religion destroyed, writers needed to discover a new faith to follow—with art often filling the void. In his preface to *The Nigger of Narcissus*, Conrad wrote: "Art itself may be defined as a single-minded attempt to render the highest kind of justice to the visible universe, by bringing to light the truth, manifold and one, underlying its very aspect." For him, art was religion.

New techniques emerged for novelists to tell their stories. The stream of consciousness and internal monologue emphasized a shift in focus from the external world to the interior world. Dreams, thoughts, and explanations of a character's mental process replaced lengthy descriptions of external objects. Even though Conrad did not use these devices per se, he did focus on the internal world of his characters, and the reality of their dreams and thoughts. Marlow's story suggests a nightmarish journey into the unknown.

More than any other factor, the advent and progression of psychology shaped the new vision of man in the universe, as well as the artist's conception of him. Freud's ideas showed the different aspects of man's personality. With Freud's analysis, man is not easily understood unless we consider his multi-layered make-up. His terms "ego," "id," and "super-ego" reveal the depth of our conscious and subconscious mind. After Freud's work appeared, many works received a "psychological" interpretation. This added a depth of meaning to each work which had not existed before.

If we look at *Heart of Darkness* specifically and apply Freud's concept of the human psyche, we can analyze Marlow's journey not only as a literal one, but a psychological one. Marlow and Kurtz represent different aspects of man's personality. Marlow reflects the "ego" (man's more rational side), while Kurtz represents the "id" (man's primitive force within). This difference explains why Marlow recoils at Kurtz's barbaric behavior.

The recurring symbols in Conrad's work show Jung's influence. Many things represent not only their actual meaning, but a symbolic one, as well. The jungle, Marlow's journey, and even Kurtz himself suggest other ideas and meanings besides their literal ones. Since Conrad gives no clues, the reader must interpret each one.

Bergson's theories of time relate to Conrad's use of a non-chronological narration. He could have had Marlow tell his story without any alteration in time, by starting at the beginning and proceeding straight through until the end. Instead, Conrad lets Marlow jump ahead, then return at whim. This technique merges the past with the present, making the reading more challenging. It shuffles the pieces of a strict chronological plot. As with the symbols, the reader must order the time to organize the sequence of events.

In his preface to *The Nigger of the Narcissus*, Joseph Conrad wrote how an artist's (writer's) success allowed readers a "glimpse of truth for which you have forgotten to ask." He also said: "Art itself may be defined as a single-minded attempt to render the highest kind of justice to the visible universe, by bringing to light the truth, manifold and one, underlying its every aspect." In each case, notice his reference to the "truth." Here, Conrad proclaimed what his contemporaries felt. Only the artist could lead society to the truth. Only the work itself could enable society to understand the truth. The modern artists stood before their audience like prophets addressing the multitudes. The twentieth-century novelists' work represented a way for the reader to see the new reality.

Master List of Characters

"I"—*An unnamed "I" narrator.*

The Director of Companies—*Captain and owner of the boat.*

The Lawyer and The Accountant—*People on the boat in the Thames.*

Charlie Marlow—*Also on the boat. Tells the story of his journey to see Kurtz deep in the jungle.*

Kurtz—*The manager of an ivory station who has rejected conventional societal beliefs.*

Two Knitting Women—*They sit outside the outer office.*

The Doctor—*He examines Marlow before his journey.*

The Aunt—*Related to Marlow, she helps him get the appointment to the ship.*

The Swedish Captain—*The man in charge of a little sea-going steamer.*

The Accountant—*The bookkeeper who draws attention because of his neat appearance.*

The Dying Agent—*The man tormented by flies at the station.*

The Manager—*Leader of the station who survives because of his excellent health.*

The Pilgrims—*Workers who carry long staves. They want any chance to obtain ivory.*

The Brickmaker—*He does secretarial work for the Manager, but doesn't seem to make bricks.*

The Boilermaker—*A good worker who talks to Marlow about the rivets they need.*

The Manager's Uncle—*The leader of the Eldorado Exploring Expedition. He only talks to his nephew.*

The Helmsman—*A black man killed by arrows shot by the natives.*

The Russian—*Wearing bright colored clothes, he greets Marlow at Kurtz's station.*

Kurtz's Black Mistress—*The woman in the jungle. She wears many bracelets, charms, and beads.*

A Clean-Shaved Man, Kurtz's "Cousin," a Journalist—*Three men who visit Marlow after Kurtz's death. They want Kurtz's papers.*

Kurtz's Intended—*The woman in Europe who Marlow visits a year after Kurtz's death.*

Summary of the Novel

Five men sit on board the *Nellie*, a boat docked in the Thames. An unnamed narrator introduces them to the reader: the owner of the boat, a lawyer, an accountant, and Charlie Marlow, who tells the story of his journey to the African jungle.

He introduces his tale by referring to ancient times in Britain, some nineteen hundred years ago. After help from an aunt, Marlow gets a job commanding a ship for an ivory trading company. Before he leaves, he meets two knitting women and a doctor from the company who make him feel uneasy.

He sails from Europe on a French steamer. The endless coastline and the appearance of sweating and shouting black men fascinate him. After more than thirty days, he leaves the French steamer for a boat captained by a Swede. He makes it to the company's Outer Station. Rotting equipment and black slaves chained by the neck appall him. Even when he runs from the sight of them, he sees black workers starving and dying slowly. He meets the company's chief accountant, a man whose neat appearance stands out from the company's chaos. He waits ten days here. The hot weather and many flies irritate Marlow. During this time, though, the accountant mentions Mr. Kurtz, a remarkable man, a first-class ivory agent, a favorite of the Administration.

Marlow leaves the Outer Station with a white companion and a caravan of sixty blacks. Through thickets, ravines, and paths they travel two-hundred miles in fifteen days to the Central Station. Marlow finds his steamboat sunk at the bottom of the river. It will take months to repair. He meets the manager, a man Marlow dislikes because he talks without thinking. He speaks of Kurtz, saying he is ill, perhaps dead. Like the accountant, the manager praises Kurtz and reiterates his importance to the company. Marlow turns his back on the manager and concentrates on repairing his steamboat. Everywhere he looks, he notices "pilgrims," white men who carry staves and speak of nothing but ivory. A shed full of goods burns one night. While going to see it, Marlow overhears the manager speaking with another agent about Kurtz.

Marlow meets a brickmaker. He invites Marlow to his room, where he asks him many questions about Europe. As he leaves the room, Marlow sees a sketch in oils of a blindfolded woman carrying a torch. Kurtz had painted it, he says, more than a year ago.

They talk about Kurtz, the agent saying he expects him to be promoted soon. He says Kurtz and Marlow belong to the same "gang" because the same people had recommended both of them. Marlow realizes this man resents Kurtz's success.

Marlow tells the agent he needs rivets to fix the boat. When Marlow finally demands the rivets, the agent abruptly changes the subject. They do not arrive for many weeks. Marlow boards his steamer after the agent leaves. He meets a boilermaker, a good worker with a long beard. They dance on deck after Marlow tells him the rivets will come soon. Led by the manager's uncle, the Eldorado Exploring Expedition appears. Marlow overhears them speak about Kurtz. He had come downriver a few months ago with ivory, but turned back. He had left a clerk to deliver the shipment, instead. He had spoken of Kurtz's illness then, with no further word coming in the last nine months.

The rivets arrive, Marlow repairs the boat, and they resume the journey. The manager, a few pilgrims, and twenty natives accompany Marlow on the steamer. It takes two months to get close to Kurtz's station. During that time, drums roll, people howl and clap, and the jungle becomes thick and dark.

They find an abandoned hut fifty-miles below Kurtz's station. Marlow discovers a faded note, a coverless book, and a stack of firewood. Eight miles from Kurtz's station, Marlow and the manager argue over their navigation. Marlow wants to push on, but the manager urges caution. A mile and a half from their destination, the natives attack the boat. A spear kills the helmsman, who falls at Marlow's feet. They throw his body into the river, a simple funeral. They come upon a man on shore. A Russian, this "harlequin" speaks admiringly of Kurtz. He tells them of Kurtz's serious illness.

While the manager and the pilgrims go to Kurtz's house, Marlow finds out many things from the Russian about Kurtz. Kurtz had ordered the attack on the steamer, he had discovered villages, and had even tried to kill the Russian over some ivory. Most importantly, the natives worshipped Kurtz, and offered sacrifices in his name.

They bring Kurtz to the steamer on an improvised stretcher. Physically weak, Kurtz still speaks with power. The natives line the shore to watch their god leave. A black woman, Kurtz's mistress, joins them. Kurtz escapes from the steamer that evening. Marlow follows him, finally returning Kurtz to the boat. Kurtz gives Marlow a packet of papers. He dies a few days later. His last words—"The horror! The horror!"—haunt Marlow. They bury him in a muddy hole the next day.

Marlow returns to Europe. He becomes sick, running a fever. Three people call on him to retrieve Kurtz's writings. A company officer, a musician claiming to be Kurtz's cousin, and a journalist want his papers for their use. Marlow gives them unimportant documents, saving the personal ones for Kurtz's Intended.

More than a year after Kurtz's death, Marlow visits this woman. At her door, he hears Kurtz's last words ring. In a drawing room, Marlow meets her, a beautiful lady suffering over Kurtz's death. Marlow never answers her questions directly. He lies to her, saying Kurtz's last words were her name. She cries to release herself from the agony of loss. Marlow feels bad for betraying Kurtz's memory, but glad for saving the woman from the truth.

With Marlow's story ended, we return to the *Nellie*. The narrator describes Marlow sitting in the pose of a Buddha, then raises his head to the "heart of the immense darkness" in the distance.

Estimated Reading Time

Due to Conrad's complex language, the long paragraphs, and the chronological shifts in narration, *Heart of Darkness* will probably take longer to cover than another work of equal length, with an actual reading time of six to seven hours.

Heart of Darkness

Section I

New Characters:

The Director of Companies: *captain and owner of the boat*

"I": *unnamed narrator on the boat*

The Lawyer, The Accountant: *people on the boat in the Thames*

Charlie Marlow: *also on the boat; tells the story of his journey to see Kurtz deep in the jungle*

Two Knitting Women: *they sit outside the outer office*

The Doctor: *he examines Marlow before his journey*

The Aunt: *related to Marlow, she helps him get his appointment to the ship*

The Swedish Captain: *the man in charge of a little sea-going steamer*

The Company's Chief Accountant: *his neat appearance contrasts with the chaos of the station*

The Dying Agent: *the man tormented by flies at the station*

The Manager: *leader of the station who survives because of his excellent health*

The Pilgrims: *workers who carry long staves; they want any chance to obtain ivory*

06/05/2018

London Public Library
Date Due Receipt

**Help us build community,
strengthen skills and
enrich lives. Donate today!
www.lpl.ca/donate**

Check due dates to avoid late
charges. Return items to any
London Public Library location.
Renew items online: http://encore.
londonpubliclibrary.ca OR by
phone: 519-661-4600.

Items checked out to

Amin, Reham Amin Sayd

TITLE   Joseph Conrad's Heart of
darkness / text by Frank

BARCODE   32104035203357

DUE DATE   **26-Jun-2018**

Thank you for visiting the library!

The Brickmaker: *does secretarial work for the manager, but does not seem to make bricks*

The Boilermaker: *a good worker who talks to Marlow about the rivets they need*

The Manager's Uncle: *leader of the Eldorado Exploring Expedition; he speaks only to his nephew*

Summary

A boat, the *Nellie*, is docked in the Thames. Its sails are still, and the water and sea calm. An unnamed narrator, who refers to himself only as "I," introduces the people on board. Four people sit on deck besides himself: the Director of Companies, the Lawyer, the Accountant, and Marlow. The Director of Companies is their captain and host. An elderly man, the Lawyer, sits on the rug for comfort, while the Accountant plays with a box of dominoes. Finally, Marlow sits cross-legged, his arms dropped, his palms facing outward. The narrator says they "exchanged a few words lazily."

The unnamed narrator thinks of the great history of the sea, its people, and ships. He mentions Sir Francis Drake and Sir John Franklin. He recalls the *Golden Hind*, the *Erebus*, and the *Terror*—ships from the past. He mentions all the greatness, dreams, and empires of history.

The sun sets. In the distance, the lights from the Chapman lighthouse, ships, and London shine at night. Still, a lurid glare glows between London and the sky.

Marlow speaks about London, saying how it's been "one of the dark places of the earth." No one responds. The narrator tells us that Marlow is the only one who still follows the sea. He considers him to be a wanderer. Their home is the ship, their country is the sea. He says Marlow is not typical. For Marlow, when he tells a tale, its meaning is not inside like a kernel, but outside.

Suddenly, Marlow begins talking about the Romans and ancient times. He pictures the cold, fog, disease, and battles with the savage natives they had to endure. He admires their courage to face the darkness. In the posture of a Buddha, he speaks about how they used only force and violence to get what they wanted. Conquests

back then, he says, meant stealing from people who were different from you. He believes there is more needed to redeem mankind, something to "bow down before, and offer a sacrifice to...."

Marlow stops speaking. There is a long silence and no one speaks. When he starts talking again, he begins to tell a story of one of his journeys. He says it reveals something about himself.

Marlow tells of how he'd spent six years traveling on the Indian Ocean, Pacific, and China Seas before taking the journey he's talking about. When he was young, he used to point to blank spaces on maps and say, "When I grow up I will go there." He's visited most of them, except one. He calls Africa a "place of darkness." He compares the Congo river on the map to a snake: its head in the sea, its body curving over a country, and its tail in the deep of the land. As he had looked at a map in a shop window, he says he was as fascinated by this place as a bird is when it looks at a snake.

He cannot secure this job until his aunt helps him. She knows the wife of a person in the Administration. Marlow cannot believe he needs help from a woman.

Marlow tells how the company had recently discovered the death of one of their captains by a native. His name was Fresleven and his murder stemmed from an argument over some black hens. Months later, when Marlow arrives, he uncovers Fresleven's body, the grass growing over his remains.

In forty-eight hours Marlow crosses the Channel and presents himself to his employer. Knitting black wool, two women—one fat, the other thin—sit outside the office. A map on a wall pictures the world in many colors. Marlow mentions the yellow patch at dead center, his destination.

Marlow meets the secretary, signs his contract, and is told he must have a medical exam. The women continue knitting as he passes through the outer office. They watch him strangely. A young clerk shows Marlow out of the office. It is early for his exam, so Marlow and the clerk have a drink. Speaking admiringly of Africa, the clerk surprises Marlow by not going there himself. "I am not such a fool as I look," he says. At his exam, the doctor measures Marlow's head with calipers. He asks if there was any madness in Marlow's family. He also adds, "...the changes take place inside, you know."

Marlow visits his aunt to thank her and say good-bye. He finds that his aunt had recommended him as "an emissary of light, something like a lower apostle." All woman are out of touch with the truth, he says. He feels hesitant about leaving Brussels for Africa, the "center of the earth." He leaves on a slow French steamer. It stops at many ports to unload soldiers and officers. The monotonous journey lulls Marlow into a depression. Occasionally, a boat from shore paddled by blacks interrupts the boredom. The steamer passes a French man-of-war ship shelling the coastline. They deliver mail to this ship. They also learn that the sailors aboard her were dying of fever at three a day. The steamer moves on, never stopping for Marlow to get a clear impression, except for "hints of nightmares." They reach the mouth of the river in thirty days. Marlow switches to a small sea-going steamer captained by a Swede to take him farther upstream. The captain tells him he had taken a fellow Swede recently up the river. The man had hanged himself. The captain cannot answer Marlow directly when he asks why. When they reach the Outer Station, Marlow gets his first glimpse of Africa, the ivory trade, and the general waste. Broken machinery and loose rails litter the ground. Commanded by an arrogant guard, a six-man chain gang walks by with the "deathlike indifference of unhappy savages."

Shocked, Marlow turns away from them and heads for the trees. Marlow avoids an artificial hole and nearly falls into a narrow ravine before reaching the shade. Black shapes occupy the area. These diseased, starving men lean against trees. Marlow gives one young man a biscuit he had gotten from the Swede's ship. He takes it, but does not eat it. Another man crawls to the river to drink.

Marlow walks away from the station. He meets a white man whose fanciful appearance contrasts with the surrounding darkness. He is the Company's chief accountant. Everything about him is orderly, unlike the "muddle" around him.

Marlow spends ten days at the Outer Station. Flies buzz. A deathly sick agent is brought in. He groans continuously. A caravan also arrives. The ensuing uproar causes the accountant to say he hates the savages "to the death." With sixty men, Marlow leaves the next day for the Central Station. He has a white companion, a man who faints and catches fever. Marlow meets a white man in an unbuttoned uniform. He says he repairs roads, but Marlow sees no roads or upkeep.

After fifteen days, Marlow reaches the Central Station. He finds that the boat he was to command was wrecked at the bottom of the river. The repair job, he knows, will take months. Marlow meets the manager in a curious interview. This man has attained his position because of his good health, not his ability and performance. The manager tells Marlow he had wanted to wait for him two days before, but he couldn't because Kurtz, the Inner Station's manager, was ill. He had visited him, and the skipper of Marlow's boat tore the bottom out. Marlow says he has heard of Kurtz. The manager assures Marlow of Kurtz's value. He also adds that it will take three months to repair the boat. Disgusted, Marlow leaves angered with the manager. He sees "pilgrims," white men carrying staves. A bit later, a shed full of prints, beads, and other goods catches fire. Marlow investigates the scene. He hears two men talking. One mentions Kurtz. The other is the manager. A black man accused of starting the fire is beaten. The "brickmaker" invites Marlow to his room for a drink. Marlow does not see a "fragment of a brick anywhere." He asks Marlow about Europe and his connections there. Marlow realizes the man intends to get information. Marlow notices a sketch in oils on the wall. It is of a "woman, draped and blindfolded, carrying a lighted torch." The manager says Kurtz had painted it a year before at the Central Station.

Marlow asks about Kurtz. The manager calls Kurtz a "prodigy," and an "emissary of pity and science and progress…." He says the same people who had sent Kurtz also had recommended Marlow. They go outside. A man with a black mustache approves of beating the black native blamed for the fire. The agent follows Marlow. He doesn't want Marlow to speak badly of him to Kurtz. Marlow detests this man who, he thinks, has "nothing inside but a little loose dirt, maybe." Marlow adds how he hates a lie because it appalls him. He also says it is hard for one person to explain himself to another because, "We live, as we dream—alone."

Momentarily, the story returns to the *Nellie*. The narrator listens intently, though the others may have been sleeping. It is dark. Marlow is more voice than person.

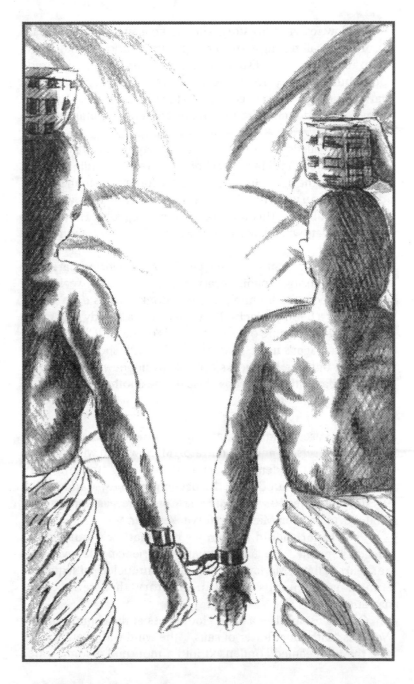

Marlow resumes his story. The brickmaker continues speaking of Kurtz, calling him a "universal genius." Marlow demands rivets to repair the boat. Every week, a caravan arrives with trade goods, but never any rivets. The man says Kurtz, too, needs rivets. Marlow suggests that, as secretary to the manager, he should find a way to obtain them. The man mentions a hippopotamus, then leaves.

Marlow needs rivets to continue. He says he does not like to work, but enjoys finding himself, his "own reality," while working. He returns to the boat. He speaks with the foreman, a man Marlow admires because of his dedication to work. A widower with six young children, this man raves about pigeons. He tells the man that rivets will arrive in a few weeks. They dance with joy on the deck.

The rivets do not come for awhile. An exploring party, the Eldorado Exploring Expedition, arrives. For the next six weeks, they appear in sections. A white man on a donkey leads each group, followed by a band of blacks. They are reckless, greedy, and cruel. They will "tear treasure out of the bowels of the land."

The manager's uncle leads them. Fat, with short legs, he resembles a butcher. He speaks only to his nephew. They stay together all day with their heads close to one another.

Analysis

Conrad uses a "framed" narrative technique. One narrator, in this case "I," sets up another narrator, Marlow, who will continue the story. At first, readers may suspect that "I" will narrate the story. He doesn't. After introducing the passengers to us, Marlow talks. His story becomes *Heart of Darkness*. Conrad reveals some of "I's" thoughts to us, then Marlow's story takes over.

The reader should remember that Marlow's journey has already happened. He is not actually experiencing the events as he speaks of them. Marlow also abandons chronological sequence. Sometimes he jumps ahead in his story, then retraces his narration.

Conrad establishes a calm gloominess at the beginning. The *Nellie* is "without a flutter of sails," "the wind was nearly calm," and the air "seemed condensed into a mournful gloom." Later,

when the sun sets, there is still a "brooding gloom in the sunshine." These descriptions suggest an eerie setting, as if something evil is about to occur. The narrator says the passengers feel "the bond of the sea" between them. We see this shared feeling when the narrator thinks of the sea's history on the Thames, and Marlow speaks of the Romans nineteen hundred years ago. The past interests them. Marlow's idea of history, though, includes the savages in Ancient Rome and "aggravated murder on a great scale." The dark side intrigues him. His first sentence contains the words "dark places." Even the river on a map resembles a snake, a sinister reptile.

Conrad deepens Marlow's uniqueness with his physical posture. He sits cross-legged in "the pose of a Buddha preaching in European clothes." Very simply, Buddhist philosophy establishes suffering as inseparable from existence. It also contains "nirvana," a state of illumination. If he imitates a Buddha, how has Marlow suffered and what does he know?

He refers to the company he will join when he calls them "conquerors," people who "grabbed what they could get for the sake of what was to be got." He disapproves of them. Since they did not have "belief in the idea," Marlow rejects their ambitions as a mere materialistic hunt.

As the traffic in London continues, the narrator mentions the green, red, and white flames gliding in the river during the "deepening night." Again, images of light and dark play against each other.

In order for Marlow to convey meaning in his tale, he says he must tell us how he got there, what he saw, and how he went up the river to meet the "poor chap," Kurtz. The journey was not "very clear," but it seemed to "throw a kind of light." In a symbolic way now, dark and light mix. Marlow relates his feelings as a child, when he used to stare at maps and dream of explorations. Since then, many of those places had been visited, named, and inhabited. One place remains, though—the river "resembling an immense snake uncoiled." Traditionally, snakes symbolize evil. Marlow speaks of it with this meaning, saying the place "had become a place of darkness." This refers to the Belgian Congo.

Marlow tells how he needed help from his aunt to secure his appointment. He says, "Then would you believe it?—I tried the women. I, Charlie Marlow, set the women to work—to get a job. Heavens!" This information seems insignificant. It isn't. Conrad foreshadows Marlow's lie to Kurtz's Intended at the end of the novel. He will sacrifice the truth for a woman.

Our first indication of wasteful suffering during Marlow's journey comes when he mentions Fresleven's death. Killed in a fight over two black hens, the captain's murder suggests an abandonment of rational behavior. Since Marlow has been to the jungle, he says it "didn't surprise me in the least to hear this." No respect is even shown to Fresleven's corpse, because Marlow discovers his body with grass growing over it.

The two knitting women present another sign of the macabre. Marlow thinks of them "guarding the door of Darkness, knitting black wool as for a warm pall..." Everything about them gives him an "eerie feeling."

Marlow's visit to the doctor adds to the idea on the unknown. The doctor measures his head, then asks if there was any sign of madness in Marlow's family. He also says the changes take place "inside." These clues lead us to believe that Marlow's journey is more than a physical one, it is a mental and psychological one.

Marlow knows what happens, but he has not told us yet. Conrad withholds information to create suspense. Though short, Marlow's visit to his aunt contains an important passage. She had recommended him, Marlow believes, using the words "emissary of light." This connects to a scene later in Section I, when the manager refers to Kurtz as an "emissary." They share the description of being a messenger or agent. We cannot know their message, though, until Marlow concludes his story.

The beginning of Marlow's journey on the French steamer initiates his descent into "darkness." They travel on the "edge of a colossal jungle, so dark as to be almost black...." At this point, light still shows. The sun is "fierce," the land "seemed to glisten," and "grayish-whitish specks showed up clustered inside the white surf." Conrad alternates images of light and darkness not only to convey mood, but to allude to ethical questions of good and bad, and right and wrong. As Marlow's journey progresses though, light fades and darkness dominates.

The Swede's story of a fellow Swede's suicide advances the idea of irrational acts. Marlow is not told the reason why he had hanged himself. We can sense the feeling of chaos Marlow will find in Africa. Why is there killing and madness? Notice how Conrad hints at these strange events without actually revealing too much about them.

Marlow notices more decay. He sees an "undersized railway truck lying on its back," the "carcass of some animal," and "a stack of rusty nails." These images define a general sense of squalor, a sign of neglect and waste. As Marlow tells of his travels, he never fails to include these descriptions. He has seen a world few of us have.

The next scene, when Marlow sees the black slaves chained together, shows us his disgust of man's treatment toward his fellow man. Here, Conrad attacks imperialism—the use by one group or nation over another for their own gain. The whites in the jungle use the blacks, reducing them to machines. Marlow feels guilty of this attitude, saying he is "a part of the great cause of these high and just proceedings." He flees from them to disassociate himself from the treatment of the blacks. But Marlow cannot run away. Everywhere, starving and dying blacks lean for rest, crawl for water, and crouch for shade. Marlow is "horrorstruck." The savage cruelty reflects the depravity in the jungle. And, he has only begun his journey.

The appearance of the Company's chief accountant represents a sharp contrast. His "brushed hair," "starched collars," and "got-up shirt-fronts" show a sense of order amidst all disorder. Marlow acknowledges him. While all around the manager falls to waste and rots, he keeps himself and his books in "apple-pie order." He cannot tolerate the groans of a dying agent in his office because it makes it "difficult to guard against clerical errors."

Marlow hears of Kurtz for the first time. The manager praises him. Marlow knows nothing of him at this time. Remember, in reality, Marlow knows everything about Kurtz because he is recounting the events, not experiencing them now.

The next part of Marlow's journey, with a caravan of sixty men, leads him through "networks of paths." No people are around, "nobody, not a hut." He sees "abandoned villages" and "ruins of grass

walls." The jungle gets darker, the isolation more pronounced. The "white men with long staves" in their hands who appear momentarily represent the "pilgrims," the ivory hunters. They seek money and profit. They ignore the degradation. Marlow's meeting with the manager here serves three purposes: he finds out that the steamer he is to command is stuck, he hears more about Kurtz, and he comes to dislike this man because he is a "chattering idiot." The manager's superior health contrasts with the information about Kurtz's illness. We should observe how Conrad's conception of health includes the physical and mental. The jungle, its weather, and isolation affect everyone in many ways. The accountant and this manager seem to have survived the conditions. Others succumb. Which group will Marlow and Kurtz belong to? The manager is an interesting character. He seems to hate Kurtz. If Marlow and Kurtz are linked together, then he must hate Marlow. This explains why Marlow is uneasy around him.

Marlow feels that the manager can only "keep the routine going—that's all." The manager never offers food or rest to Marlow. "Being hungry," he says, "and kept on my feet too, I was getting savage." The key word is, of course, "savage." Are the surroundings influencing Marlow? And if the manager praises Kurtz, but Marlow dislikes the manager, can he accept his assessment of Kurtz?

Marlow sees more "pilgrims," who speak of ivory. The word "rang in the air, was whispered, was sighed." He detests this greed for wealth. He considers it to be "philanthropic pretense." Unconcerned with money, Marlow is the outsider, the intruder.

The brickmaker's appearance poses an intriguing question. How can he be a brickmaker if there are no bricks around? He fits the man who repairs roads earlier in the section, when Marlow said he did not see roads or upkeep. A mysterious element surrounds many characters. It is difficult to get a sense of them. Conrad leaves us questioning both who these people are, and Marlow's description of them. Are they the way Marlow describes them, or is he purposely omitting important information about them? If he is, then why? Conrad raises these questions through the use of the first-person flashback narrative.

Marlow's description of Kurtz's oil painting gives us the first solid detail about him. The picture of a woman draped and blindfolded carrying a lighted torch against a black background suggests a few ideas. First, we see the combination of light and dark again. The blindfold refers to the actual darkness, as well as a spiritual and philosophical one, since the person cannot "see." The woman anticipates Kurtz's mistress and Intended, two women who will appear later.

In the next sequence, Marlow reveals much about his philosophy. He says he hates and detests a lie. Again, Conrad foreshadows the ending, when Marlow lies to Kurtz's Intended. Later, we have to compare that moment with this statement. Marlow then says it is difficult for him to convey Kurtz to his listeners, the people on the boat. This implies us, the reader, also. "Do you see him? Do you see the story? Do you see anything? It seems to me I am trying to tell you a dream." he says. This points to Marlow's problem. He is trying to tell the untellable, explain the unexplainable. Marlow's words reflect Conrad's function as a writer—to make the reader understand the story. "We live, as we dream—alone." Marlow adds. This statement comes close to illuminating Marlow's tale. It is extremely difficult, if not impossible, for one person to understand another.

If this is true, then Marlow cannot understand Kurtz, Kurtz cannot understand Marlow, and we cannot understand either of them. We can try to make sense, nothing more. As Marlow's tale becomes philosophical, Conrad takes us back to the *Nellie* and the "I" narrator. This breaks the dream-like trance of the story. We come back to reality, if only for a moment. Everyone but the narrator is asleep. If we are like him, then we are "on watch for the sentence, for the word, that would give…the clue" to this story. Together, we try to catch Marlow's meaning.

Conrad returns to Marlow's story and a most practical matter: the need for rivets. Without them, his journey ends. This leads to a humorous scene when Marlow meets the Boilermaker, one of the few men he admires in the jungle. They reassure themselves that the rivets will arrive in three weeks, then danced "like lunatics."

The Eldorado Exploring Expedition arrives. Marlow abhors them. They want to "tear treasure out of the bowels of the land." They represent the greedy white men, whose sole purpose revolves around destroying the land to obtain money and wealth. Since

the manager's uncle leads them, they further the idea of the pilgrims' infiltration. They lack "moral purpose," something Marlow
appreciates.

Instead, Marlow thinks of Kurtz, a man "who had come out
equipped with moral ideas of some sort." His interest stimulated,
Marlow begins the next step on his quest to the mysterious ivory
agent and the heart of darkness, a mythical place of hell.

Study Questions

1. Identify the people on the *Nellie*.

2. Why is it ironic that Marlow needs his aunt's help to secure
   his appointment?

3. What happened to Fresleven, one of the Company's captains?

4. How are the two women outside the secretary's office symbolic?

5. Name two unusual procedures at Marlow's physical exam.

6. How did the Swede die?

7. What is unique about the chief accountant's appearance?

8. Why was the manager successful at his job?

9. Why does Marlow call some people on the boat "pilgrims"?

10. Why does Marlow need the brickmaker's help?

Answers

1. A narrator, a company director, a lawyer, an accountant, and
   Marlow are aboard the *Nellie*.

2. It is ironic that Marlow needs his aunt's help because she is
   a woman in a male-dominated world, the sea.

3. Fresleven was murdered by a native in a quarrel over black
   hens.

4. The women outside the secretary's office knit black wool,
   the symbol of death.

5. The doctor measures Marlow's head with calipers, and asks if there has been madness in his family.

6. The Swede hanged himself.

7. The chief accountant is neat and orderly.

8. The manager was successful because he was always healthy.

9. Marlow calls them "pilgrims" because they carry staves and their "pilgrimage" is to obtain ivory.

10. Marlow need rivets from the brickmaker to repair the boat.

Suggested Essay Topics

1. From the very opening on the Thames in *Heart of Darkness,* when day mixes with night, Conrad uses images of light and dark. Traditionally, light represents "good" and dark represents "bad." Does Conrad use these interpretations in the same way? What do his constant references to light and dark suggest about Marlow's story? Remember, Africa is the "dark continent," where the black natives live.

2. Conrad alters his narration by making Marlow jump back and forth in time. Marlow mentions people and events we won't know about until later. Cite examples when he does this, and explain how it affects the story. What advantages are there in breaking the sequence of events? Why does he tell us some things, while withholding others?

3. In a sense, two narrators speak—a nameless "I" and Charlie Marlow. The narrator introduces Marlow, then tells us some of his ideas. When Marlow speaks, we see everything from his perspective. Suppose someone else told Marlow's story? Say, perhaps, the narrator or, possibly, one of the people Marlow meets along his journey. How would the story change? Would the information and details be different?

4. After taking the steamer captained by the Swede, Marlow sees the blacks for the first time. Why does the sight of them appall him? Why is he bothered by the way they are treated? No one else seems to be disturbed by their condition, so why is Marlow?

5. Section I contains a number of shorter episodes, as Marlow switches steamers and heads deeper into the jungle. What does he see and experience at each temporary stop over? Is there a progression as he moves from one boat to another? Does each stop affect Marlow's attitude and opinion toward what he sees?

SECTION THREE

Heart of Darkness

Section II

New Characters:

The Helmsman: *a black man killed by arrows shot by natives*

The Russian: *man who greets Marlow at Kurtz's station*

Summary

While on his boat, Marlow hears the manager and his uncle talk about Kurtz. They stand on the shore alongside the steamboat. Without moving, he listens. The manager fears Kurtz's influence. Threatened by Kurtz's influence and success, the manager says, "Am I the manager—or am I not?" The uncle hopes the climate will eventually ruin Kurtz.

From the "absurd sentences," Marlow hears how Kurtz had traveled three hundred miles with a shipment of ivory nine months ago. Kurtz had then returned upriver in a canoe with four native paddlers, a "half-caste" left in charge of delivering the load of ivory. Kurtz's station has been without goods and stores since then. Kurtz's motives escape the manager and his uncle. Marlow says he sees Kurtz in his mind for the first time, how he faces the wilderness and desolation. The half-caste, a "scoundrel" to the manager and his uncle, had told of Kurtz's illness and how he had "recovered imperfectly." They walk away from Marlow, then return close to the boat again. When they speak this time, Marlow is not sure if they are talking about Kurtz, or about someone else in Kurtz's district of whom the manager disapproves. The manager says neither of them will be free until "one of these fellows is hanged." They agree that the real danger begins in Europe, where the orders come from. The manager quotes something Kurtz had said: "Each station should be like a beacon on the road towards better things, a center for trade of course, but also for humanizing, improving, instructing." He calls Kurtz an "ass" for his ideas and his desire to be a manager one day. The uncle reassures his nephew when he says, "...I say, trust to this." He points to the jungle around him while he speaks, as if to say all these things will help you destroy Kurtz. Marlow jumps up to look at the forest, half expecting to receive an answer from the darkness. They knew he had been listening, he says, because they went back to the station "pretending not to know anything of my existence." Side by side, they walk away, their unequal shadows trailing behind them. The Eldorado Expedition leaves for the wilderness a few days later. In the future, Marlow finds out all the donkeys died, as well as the blacks, "the less valuable animals."

Marlow is excited about meeting Kurtz soon. It will not happen for two more months, though. They encounter warm air, empty streams, and the deep forest as they travel upriver. Marlow compares it to going back to the beginning of the world. Hippos and alligators line the sand-banks. Stillness and silence brood over everything. He has to watch for hidden banks to avoid damaging the boat. He looks for wood to burn for the next day's steaming. He refers to the details of his job as "monkey tricks," as the mysterious Truth watches him. He says when you attend to things on the surface, reality fades. The inner truth, he adds, is "hidden—luckily."

For a moment, we return to the men aboard the *Nellie*. One man says, "Try to be civil, Marlow." The narrator knows one person besides himself is listening. Driving the boat, Marlow says, resuming his story, was like a "blindfolded man set to drive a van over a bad road." He sweats and shivers over worrying about the boat. Once, he needs twenty cannibals to help push the boat. With sarcasm and humor, he says they at least did not "eat each other before my face." He recalls the smell of rotten hippo-meat the cannibals had brought with them. With the manager and three or four pilgrims holding their staves aboard, they pass white men greeting them with joy about ivory, the word itself ringing in the air. Massive trees fill the immense landscape. Marlow's journey is now headed "towards Kurtz—exclusively." He is not sure who it crawls to for the pilgrims. He hears the roll of drums, but does not understand if they signify war, peace, or prayer. The snapping of a twig can shatter the stillness of dawn. He again compares his journey to prehistoric times. Ancient man curses, prays, and welcomes them. Like phantoms, they glide past their surroundings. When natives howl and leap, Marlow thinks not how different they are from him, but their "remote kinship" to him. He says it is "ugly," if you are at least willing to admit it. He philosophizes about man's mind, and how it encompasses all periods of time and knowledge. Man must meet the truth with his own strength, not an external force.

Someone on the *Nellie* grunts a question. Marlow answers by saying he did not go ashore because he had to worry about the steampipes and the boat. Marlow mentions the fireman, a black man who keeps fire in the boiler. He could have been on shore with the natives, but instead helps Marlow because he has been trained for a profession. His filed teeth, strange patterns shaved on his head, and three scars on each of his cheeks fit well with his belief that an evil spirit lived inside the boiler. Both Marlow and the fireman are too busy with their jobs to think about their "creepy thoughts."

Marlow reaches a reed hut fifty miles below the Inner Station, Kurtz's domain. He finds a stack of firewood and a note: "Wood for you. Hurry up. Approach cautiously." Marlow knows something is wrong, but is not sure what. They look into the jungle, but find no clues. In the hut, with a plank on two posts serving as a table and rubbish in a dark corner, he finds a coverless book, *An Inquiry into some Points of Seamanship* . He handles it with care, even though it is not an "enthralling book." Marlow appreciates the work and concern required to write it. Finding the book and looking at the notes in cipher along the margin equal an "extravagant mystery" for Marlow.

While absorbed with the book, Marlow forgets the forest, the manager, and woodpile. When he looks up, everything has gone.

The pilgrims shout at him, as he puts the book in his pocket. The boat is loaded and ready to go. The manager calls the white man who had lived in the hut an "intruder." He assumes he is English, but this will not protect him from trouble unless he is careful. No one in the world is safe from trouble, Marlow observes with "assumed innocence."

Convinced the more rapid current will overpower the steamer, Marlow expects the boat to give "her last gasp." Somehow, though, it moves on. Marlow thinks of what he will say to Kurtz when he meets him. Then he experiences a "flash of insight," and realizes the importance of this affair is under the surface, beyond his understanding.

In two days they are eight miles from Kurtz's station. The manager suggests they wait until morning for safety. Annoyed, Marlow reasons that one more night means little after so many months. The unnatural silence makes him believe he is deaf. At three in the morning, fish leap, their splash reminding Marlow of gun fire. Fog accompanies the rising sun. It lifts by eight or nine in the morning. He orders the anchor, which they were taking in, to be paid out again. A clamor "modulated in savage discords" through the air. It ends in a shriek, then stops, leaving silence. Frightened, the pilgrims rush for their guns—Winchesters. They anticipate an attack.

Marlow notices the different expressions on the whites and blacks aboard the ship. The whites look discomposed, shocked at the frightful noise. Though interested, the blacks remain calm. They grunt to each other. One black man says they should catch the people hiding in the jungle. When Marlow asks why, he says, "Eat 'im!" Bothered at first by this idea, Marlow figures they are hungry. Besides some rations they had brought aboard, they had taken only rotten hippo-meat, which the pilgrims had thrown overboard. In theory, Marlow says, they were to use their payment—three nine-inch pieces of brass—to purchase food at the villages. They could not, though, because there were no villages, the people were hostile, or the manager did not want to stop. Sarcastically, Marlow says they could have eaten the wire itself for food. Marlow wonders why the cannibals do not eat the five white men. They could have easily overpowered them. Something had restrained them, but Marlow is not sure what. He and the others look "unwholesome" and "un-appetizing," he concludes. He also believes starvation is easier to fight than "bereavement, dishonor, and perdition of one's soul...." Fighting hunger requires all of a man's strength.

The manager wants to push on. Marlow knows they cannot steer properly. The manager authorizes him to "take all the risks." Marlow refuses. The manager defers to his judgment. Marlow turns away from the manager to look into the fog. He compares the adventures in approaching Kurtz to an "enchanted princess sleeping in a fabulous castle." The manager fears an attack. Marlow believes the thick fog will prevent it. He associates "sorrow" with the natives, not violence. Marlow feels the pilgrims stare at him as if he is mad. He watches the fog the way a "cat watches a mouse." Marlow interprets the natives' actions as protective and desperate, not aggressive or even defensive.

They travel through the thick fog until they come within a mile and a half below Kurtz's station. A bright green islet appears in the middle of the stream. Marlow can steer either left or right, with each path looking similar. He chooses the western passage because he had been informed the station was on the west side. It is narrower than he had anticipated. He steers the boat close to the bank, where the water is deepest. Marlow mentions the helmsman, a black man who thinks highly of himself. He wears a pair of brass earrings and blue cloth wrapper. When Marlow is next to him, this man steers with "no end of a swagger," but if no one is near he falls "prey to an abject funk." Marlow looks at the sounding-pole sticking further out of the water each time the poleman puts it in. This indicates how the water turns shallow.

The next moment, the poleman falls flat to the deck without the pole, and the fireman sits ducking by his furnace. Arrows fly. Marlow instructs the helmsman to steer straight. The pilgrims fire their guns into the jungle. Letting go of the steering, the helmsman grabs a gun. Marlow yells at him to return to his duty. He may have as well "ordered a tree not to sway in the wind." Instead, he steers the boat toward the bank. They hit overhanging bushes.

The helmsman holds his rifle and yells at the shore. Something big appears in the air, knocking the helmsman back. His head hits the wheel twice. He rolls back and stares up at Marlow, a shaft of

spear sticking below his ribs. He lands at Marlow's feet. The helmsman's blood fills Marlow's shoes. The helmsman clutches the spear while Marlow forces himself to turn away from him and steer. He pulls the steam whistle cord repeatedly with one hand. The warlike yells die, the arrows stop.

Marlow and a pilgrim in pink pajamas stand over the helmsman. He dies without making a sound, a frown coming over his face at the last moment. Marlow tells the agent to steer. He tugs at his shoelaces. He believes Kurtz is dead now, too. Marlow throws one shoe overboard. He feels disappointment in not being able to speak with Kurtz now. Even though he had heard Kurtz was a swindler and thief, Marlow feels he is still a "gifted creature." Kurtz's ability to talk still fascinates him. He throws his other shoe overboard. Marlow thinks he has missed his destiny in life if he cannot hear Kurtz talk. He feels more lonely than if he had been "robbed of a belief."

On the *Nellie*, Marlow lights his pipe. The match shows his narrow face and dropped eyelids. He draws on his pipe, then the match goes out. This momentary switch in scene ends.

Marlow speaks of missing the privilege of listening to Kurtz. He amazes himself that he does not shed tears over missing Kurtz. He considers Kurtz "very little more than a voice." The "I" narrator cuts in again, telling us that Marlow becomes silent for a long time. We return quickly to Marlow's story. Marlow now jumps ahead in his story. He mentions women, specifically Kurtz's Intended, who will not appear until the end of the novella, after Marlow returns from Africa. He says she is "out of it," meaning out of touch with all that happened in Africa. He talks of Kurtz's baldness, an "ivory ball" of a head. Marlow marvels at the amount of ivory Kurtz had collected. It fills the mud shanty and the boat when they load it. There could not be a single tusk either above or below the ground. He says Kurtz watched over it and referred to everything as belonging to him.

Speaking philosophically, Marlow says Kurtz belonged to the "powers of darkness." He adds how Kurtz sat "amongst the devils of the land...." He tells about Kurtz's background, how he had been educated in England with a half-English mother and a half-French father. He says all "Europe contributed to the making of Kurtz." He finds out how Kurtz had been instructed by the International Society for the Suppression of Savage Customs to write a report. Marlow sees it later, seventeen pages written before Kurtz's nerves "went wrong." A beautiful piece of writing, it described Kurtz presiding at midnight dances with unspeakable rites.

Marlow recalls Kurtz's words. In one section, Kurtz had written how the blacks approach the whites as if they possess the "might as of a deity...." He also had written "Exterminate all the brutes." Marlow considers the writing to be the "unbounded power of words." He tells how Kurtz believed his pamphlet would secure his future career. Kurtz was not common, Marlow says. His power to charm had influenced the natives, as well as himself. He cannot forget him, yet he is not sure it was worth the helmsman's death to reach him.

Marlow ends his jump ahead in the story, the "flash-forward." He returns to the helmsman's death. Marlow misses the helmsman and the partnership they had developed as they worked together. The bond now broken, he remembers the "profundity" of the helmsman's look before he had died. Marlow puts on dry slippers, then throws the helmsman's body overboard. The current takes his body, it rolls over twice, then disappears. Marlow says he had been a second-rate helmsman, but now he would be a first-class temptation—meaning food for the cannibals. Marlow steers after the funeral. Everyone on board believes Kurtz is dead. One red-haired pilgrim says they must have slaughtered everyone. Marlow says they at least had made a lot of smoke. He thinks they had missed their targets during the fight, by shooting too high. The screeching whistle had sent them running, he maintains. The manager talks of getting down the river for safety before it turns dark.

A decaying building with the jungle background fills the slope of a hill. They finally see the station. A white man wearing a hat like a cartwheel motions to them. Other human forms glide through the jungle. Marlow stops the engine and lets the boat drift. The manager tells the man about the attack. The man knows about it and says everything is all right. He reminds Marlow of a harlequin: bright clothes of blue, red, and yellow sparkling in the sun. He looks young with a boyish face, no beard, and little blue eyes. He asks Marlow if he is English, and Marlow answers with the same question. Pointing up the hill, he tells them Kurtz is there. Armed, the manager and pilgrims go to the house. The man comes aboard. He says the whistle will scare the natives, "simple people," he calls them. The sound of the whistle works better to drive the natives away than guns do, he says. People don't talk to Mr. Kurtz, he adds, they listen to him. The son of an arch-priest, he is Russian, had run away from school, and served on English ships. He had been wandering alone on the river for two years. He is twenty-five, not so young as he looks. He tells Marlow the small house, stack of wood, and note were his. Marlow hands him the book. He makes as if to kiss Marlow, but restrains himself. Marlow finds out that the notes in the book are in Russian, not cipher. He tells Marlow that the natives had attacked because they do not want Kurtz to be taken away, not to kill him and the crew. Kurtz has "enlarged" his mind, he adds. He opens his arms and stares at Marlow.

Analysis

Marlow hears second-hand information about Kurtz from the manager and his uncle. Their opinion of him contrasts Marlow's growing admiration for Kurtz. He gathers bits from them about Kurtz, the way we gather bits from him. He anticipates meeting Kurtz, mirroring our interest. Their fear of Kurtz and his success parallels Marlow's desire to meet him and draw his own conclusions. Marlow understands Kurtz's fine business sense when the manager talks of the ivory, "lots of it," coming from Kurtz's station. This period establishes Marlow's changing reason for his journey. At first, it was for the job and the adventure, but now Kurtz occupies his thoughts. He says he seemed "to see Kurtz for the first time." Surrounded by paddling savages, Kurtz leads the way "towards the depth of the wilderness." At this time, Marlow does not understand Kurtz's rejection of conventional society for unknown territory.

We come to see how the manager and his uncle represent the selfishness and greediness of civilized Europe. They care only about themselves, their positions, and promotions. They ridicule Kurtz's philosophy of how each station should be a "beacon on the road towards better things, a center for trade of course, but also for humanizing, improving, instructing." Kurtz's idyllic vision aggra-

vates them. Ironically, we will find out how Kurtz's life and prac-
tices contrast with his once idealistic views. When the manager's
uncle asks him if he feels well, we see the power of the jungle, as it
weakens and kills people. The uncle gestures toward the forest as
he suggests how the climate may destroy Kurtz. Marlow calls the
man's wishes a "treacherous appeal to the lurking death, to the
hidden evil, to the profound darkness of its heart." Physically, the
jungle conquers most men, leaving only the strong to live on. The
power of nature overwhelms the power of man.

Marlow then compares traveling farther into the jungle to prehistoric times. The "empty stream," "great silence," and "impen-
etrable forest" validate this association. No civilization or laws
governed people then. Marlow recalls his own past "in the shape
of an unrestful and noisy dream, remembered with wonder
amongst the overwhelming realities of this strange world of plants,
and water, and silence." As he journeys deeper into the forest, reality fades. A dream-like quality, with its "inner truth" surfaces. He
adds to this idea of the ancient past without laws by speaking of
the cannibals on the boat. These "fine fellows" show their progression to modern man by working well and not eating each other in
front of Marlow. As civilized and tamed people, they fit Marlow's
European view of man, not the native African, which he speaks of
next. As the drums roll, Marlow sees the natives on shore. Their
howling, leaping, and spinning thrill him. Their behavior evokes a
"remote kinship with this wild and passionate roar." Instead of re-
jecting their outbursts, Marlow identifies with them; he understands that part in himself. Since the "mind of man is capable of
anything," Marlow intellectually merges past and present.

This enables him to meet the truth before him—these savages
dancing in the jungle. Notice how the farther he moves away from
Europe, the more he identifies with the natives. The fireman, who
fires the boiler, represents a combination of both worlds, savage
and civilized. Marlow says he "ought to have been clapping his
hands and stamping his feet on the bank." Physically, he resembles
a typical native. He wears a charm made of rags around his arm
and a piece of polished bone through his lower lip. He considers
the fire in the boiler to be an "evil spirit." Since "he had been instructed," though, he works on the boat. He personifies the trans-

formation from the savage native to the educated white man. Marlow compares him to a dog walking on his hind-legs, which simultaneously insults and compliments him.

The hut they come upon some fifty miles below the Inner Station foreshadows Marlow's meeting with the Russian and a packet of papers Kurtz will give him. We find out at the end of Section II of *Heart of Darkness* that the Russian had left the note, firewood, and book. Marlow handles the coverless book, *An Inquiry into some Points of Seamanship*, "with the greatest possible tenderness." A plain book, this work attracts Marlow because it represents "an honest concern for the right way of going to work." He appreciates the care necessary to write it. He compares having to stop reading to tearing himself "away from the shelter of an old and solid friendship." Later, in Section III, when Kurtz hands Marlow his personal papers, Marlow will handle them with extreme care, too. Their value transcends their tattered appearance.

As the boat progresses up the river, Marlow and the manager disagree about their navigation. The manager urges caution, while Marlow wants to push on. Fearing the warning alluded to in the Russian's note, the manager suggests traveling in daylight for safety. Yearning "to talk openly with Kurtz," Marlow intends to get there as quickly as possible. Any delay annoys him. He disregards the dangers.

Marlow returns to the idea of the savage cannibals. They belong to the beginnings of time and eat rotten hippo-meat. He marvels at how they simply do not overpower the white men to eat them. For all their supposed barbarity, the savages and cannibals control their behavior more than the white man, who initiates violence in the search for ivory and wealth. The cannibals' "primitive honor" restrains them from physical aggression. They even check their hunger through some kind of restricting code of law. The arguments between Marlow and the manager build the tension and accentuate their differences. Since Marlow thinks of Kurtz as "an enchanted princess sleeping in a fabulous castle," he wants to avoid caution and further delays. The closer Marlow gets to Kurtz, the more reckless he becomes. The manager always remains wary. Marlow's personal quest interferes with the manager's business-like approach. The forest turns thickest within a mile and a half of

Kurtz's station. Trees stand in "serried ranks," twigs overhang the "current thickly," and a "broad strip of shadow" falls across the water.

Conrad intends this blurring on literal and symbolic levels. While the vegetation prevents Marlow from seeing the natives in the jungle, man's humanity and morality mix with his inhumanity and immorality. It becomes difficult to distinguish one from the other. The jungle disguises man's external and internal worlds. The densely matted forest allows the natives to attack Marlow's boat. Marlow sees "human limbs in movement" in the "tangled gloom," but cannot prepare for the arrows. The pilgrims, with their more sophisticated weapons, lose any advantage they might have. Accustomed to the jungle, the natives seize the initiative with their primitive spears. The pilgrims fire at random into the forest. They cannot see their targets, but their targets can see them. The helmsman's death in battle establishes Marlow's growing obsession with meeting Kurtz.

The helmsman suffers a horrible death, a spear hitting him in the side below the ribs. He spills a pool of blood onto the floor and Marlow's feet. After watching him die, Marlow thinks that Kurtz must be dead as well. "For the moment that was the dominant thought," he adds, showing his disregard for the helmsman's life. This man means little to him in relation to Kurtz. Later, he checks himself by saying that meeting Kurtz may not have been "exactly worth the life we lost in getting to him." When Marlow next considers Kurtz to "present himself as a voice," we see how Conrad connects him to Kurtz. In Section I, the narrator had said Marlow telling his story "had been no more to us than a voice." The way we listen to Marlow parallels the way Marlow listens to Kurtz. Marlow believes Kurtz to be "something altogether without substance." This is what Marlow is for us, the reader—merely a voice speaking words. Of course, Conrad throws in a catch. There is "substance" to Kurtz's story and Marlow's story. Marlow must interpret Kurtz's words, while we must interpret Marlow's words. These comparisons determine important distinctions. Marlow is like Kurtz because he leads, but he also resembles us because he listens.

Next, Conrad interrupts Marlow's story to return to the *Nellie*. These transitions accomplish two things: one, they force us to

listen more intently; two, they break the dream-like quality of Marlow's journey by bringing us back to the reality of the present on the boat. The first time, Marlow lights his pipe, which illuminates his face momentarily. The second time, Marlow becomes silent. The idea of light and dark couples with sound and silence. The alternating shades of white and black suggest the good and evil of the actions of Marlow's company toward the natives, the changing shades in the jungle, and the white Europeans and the black Africans. The sound and silence reflect the intermittent noises in the jungle, and Kurtz's voice in life against his silence in death for Marlow.

Marlow then jumps forward in his narrative. By breaking the chronological structure, Conrad again forces us to listen to Marlow's suggestion of looking beneath the surface to understand the finer points of his tale. We cannot simply accept the story as told, but must consider how Conrad gives us information. The deception Conrad incorporates in his narrative mirrors the deception Marlow encounters in the jungle. While he navigates the Congo, we navigate his story.

One oversight affects the rest of the journey/story. In his jump ahead, Marlow offers us glimpses of Kurtz before he appears. First, he mentions Kurtz's Intended, the woman who waits for him in Europe. She will not appear until the end of the novella. He covets ivory, with his bald head even summoning the image of "an ivory ball." He refers to everything as "my," and belongs to the powers of darkness. Kurtz represents evil, a connection to man's dark side. In a "high seat amongst the devils of the land," Kurtz leads the natives in literal and symbolic ways. Marlow's ambition of speaking to Kurtz shows how he wants to embrace and understand Kurtz, his world, and his philosophy. In a sense, Marlow wants to transform himself into one of the natives, a follower of this mad deity. Marlow attributes Kurtz's origin not to Africa and the jungle, but Europe. Since "all Europe contributed to the making of Kurtz," we see how Conrad rejects the idea of the black natives as evil, instead accusing the white European society of creating this devilish man. Here, Conrad flips the traditional image of white/good and black/ bad around. Appearances can be deceiving, as the jungle often proves. Kurtz's report for the International Society for the Suppression of Savage Customs enhances his relationship to the dark side. Marlow learns of the "unspeakable rites" Kurtz presided at, the sacrifices "offered up to him," and the "exterminate all the brutes" ideology he espoused. Kurtz preaches a racial inequality, with the blacks looking at the whites "in the nature of supernatural beings." Ironically, Kurtz becomes a savage while reporting for their suppression. Marlow does not say whether he approves of Kurtz's ideas, even if he admires the "unbounded power of eloquence" of the words. Confused by the contradicting images of Kurtz, Marlow thinks that "whatever he was, he was not common." He could "charm or frighten rudimentary souls."

In Section I, the narrator said "Marlow was not typical." Conrad develops another similarity, here, suggesting how Marlow charms us with his words, and frightens us with them, as well. Marlow says Kurtz will not be forgotten, which he will assure because "as it turned out, he was to have the care of his memory." Will we carry on Marlow's memory?

The appearance of the Russian next adds a sort of strange, humorous element to the story. A brightly dressed "harlequin" with blue, red, and yellow patches over all his clothes, this man announces Kurtz's presence to Marlow. He is reminiscent of the "Fool" in Shakespeare's *King Lear*, a character who looks nonsensical, yet imparts much wisdom. He speaks to Marlow while the manager and pilgrims investigate Kurtz's situation. He fills in some missing details for Marlow. He tells him that the hut, firewood, and note had been his. He explains how the natives had run for fear from the boat's whistle, adding how they "don't want him to go"—meaning Kurtz. And, most importantly for Marlow, he relates how Kurtz's speaking had captivated him. Almost as a sign of thanks for these bits of information, Marlow gives him the book he had found in the hut. The Russian returns the thanks by making to kiss Marlow, but "restrained himself." This act foreshadows Marlow's return of Kurtz's manuscript to Kurtz's Intended at the end of the novella. Marlow always handles with care the things he treasures, particularly Kurtz's memory. The Russian says Kurtz has "enlarged" his mind. Kurtz's life has answered some deep need for the Russian. Marlow's need to meet Kurtz will be answered shortly, in the next section. For the moment, though, when the Russian "opened his

arms wide," Marlow receives his long-awaited invitation to Kurtz's world. This last image alludes to a religious service, where a priest (the Russian) invites his parishioner (Marlow) to worship their god (Kurtz).

Study Questions

1. When he is on the boat, who does Marlow overhear speaking about Kurtz?

2. Why does Marlow compare the jungle to prehistoric times?

3. How does the cannibals' food affect Marlow?

4. Why does the book Marlow finds in the hut interest him?

5. Why couldn't the men aboard the boat spend their money for food?

6. Who aboard the boat is killed during the attack?

7. How does Marlow scare the natives during the fight?

8. Why does Marlow throw his shoes overboard?

9. Why does the Russian leave a note on the woodpile?

10. Why did Kurtz write a report?

Answers

1. Marlow overhears the manager and his uncle talk of Kurtz.

2. The violence, degradation, and lack of civility in the jungle remind Marlow of prehistoric times.

3. The cannibals' hippo-meat is rotten, smells, and makes Marlow think of his own hunger.

4. The book in the hut interests Marlow because it reflects a task planned and done well.

5. The men on the boat could not buy food because the manager did not stop, and/or the villages were destroyed.

6. The helmsman dies during the attack.

7. Marlow blows the steam whistle and the natives fear the noise.

8. Marlow throws his shoes overboard because they are soaked with blood from the helmsman's wounds.

9. The Russian leaves a note to tell someone to hurry and prepare for the coming danger.

10. Kurtz writes a document because he was instructed to chronicle his experience with the savages.

Suggested Essay Topics

1. Marlow hears about Kurtz when other people talk about him. The accountant, brickmaker, manager, and the manager's uncle speak of Kurtz to each other and/or Marlow. He pieces together their offhand remarks to form his opinion of Kurtz. From their references, characterize Kurtz. Is he admirable, a good ivory-agent, successful? Is it possible their positions influence their feelings toward Kurtz?

2. Marlow's journey to Africa enables him to meet for the first time the natives, people unlike him in many ways. How does Marlow, as well as the other white men, contrast with the blacks? Focus not only on their physical differences, but their behavior and general way of life. Are they representative of their distinct cultures, since one group comes from "civilized" Europe and the other comes from the "dark" continent?

3. A few times during Section I, Marlow mentions how he anticipates meeting Kurtz. Why does Kurtz intrigue him? Has the gossip about Kurtz fueled his interest? Is there any logical reason why he becomes obsessed with meeting Kurtz, a white man like himself?

4. The conversation between Marlow and the manager in Section I, and the talk between the manager and his uncle at the beginning of Section II, establish the manager's character. According to Marlow, he has no good qualities. Show how the manager is greedy, self-centered, and more of a hindrance to Marlow than a help. Remember, the manager envies Kurtz, a man Marlow longs to meet. Could this account for Marlow's unflattering picture of him?

5. Conrad ends Section I between when the manager's uncle arrives and the manager talks to his uncle about Kurtz. Section II ends right after the Russian greets Marlow and tells them preliminary information about himself and Kurtz. Why does Conrad end these sections here? Are they important breaks in the plot? Would *Heart of Darkness* have been different if Conrad had left the novella as one chapter, with no separate sections?

Heart of Darkness

Section III

New Characters:

Kurtz's Black Mistress: *black woman in the jungle who wears many ornaments*

A Clean-Shaved Man, Kurtz's "Cousin," a Journalist: *three people who visit Marlow in Europe to get Kurtz's papers*

Kurtz's Intended: *Kurtz's fiancée in Europe*

Summary

Marlow looks at the Russian, whose "improbable, inexplicable, and altogether bewildering" existence fascinates him. He wonders how he had survived in the jungle. Marlow imagines he will disappear before his eyes. The Russian tells Marlow to take Kurtz away quickly. Marlow does not envy the Russian's devotion to Kurtz because he had not "meditated over it." He believes it is a "most dangerous thing."

Marlow compares the Russian and Kurtz to ships "becalmed near each other." The Russian fulfills Kurtz's need to have an audience. He says he had talked to Kurtz many nights, especially about love. Kurtz had made him "see" things.

The Russian throws his arms up in praise of Kurtz. The headman of Marlow's wood-cutters looks at Marlow. Frightened, for the first time he sees the jungle as a dark place without hope.

The Russian's friendship with Kurtz had been broken, not continuous. He had nursed Kurtz through two illnesses. Often, he had waited many days for Kurtz to return from his wanderings.

He tells Marlow how Kurtz had discovered villages, a lake, and searched for ivory. It had always been worth the wait. Marlow reminds the Russian how Kurtz had run out of goods to trade for ivory. The Russian says, "There's a good lot of cartridges left even yet."

Marlow figures that Kurtz had raided the country. He asks if Kurtz had the natives following him. The Russian says the natives adore Kurtz, lured by his "thunder and lightning." He says Kurtz can be terrible at times, but no one can judge him as you would an ordinary man. Once, Kurtz had tried to kill him, he says. Kurtz had wanted his ivory. The Russian had given it to him. He had to be careful, until he had reestablished his friendship with Kurtz. He had nursed him through his second illness then. Marlow says Kurtz is mad. The Russian objects. He tells Marlow he will change his mind when he hears Kurtz speak.

Marlow sees people moving in the forest through his binoculars. He compares the woods to the "closed door of a prison." The silence disturbs him. The Russian tells Marlow that Kurtz is very ill now. Only lately had he come to the river, after an absence of many months. Marlow sees round knobs on posts near Kurtz's house. They are "black, dried, sunken" heads. The first one in the row faces him. It seems to smile at some "dream of that eternal slumber." Marlow believes the heads show Kurtz's lack of restraint. The wilderness had made him mad, he figures. Marlow can only wonder if Kurtz knows of his own "deficiency." He puts down his binoculars.

The Russian tells Marlow about Kurtz's ascendancy, how the chiefs venerate him, and how keeping him alive has occupied all his time. Marlow does not want to hear about the ceremonies used to honor Kurtz. Marlow believes he is in a "region of subtle horrors." The Russian justifies Kurtz's savagery by telling Marlow the heads had belonged to rebels, Kurtz's opposition. Kurtz's trying life, he adds, had led him to these cruel acts. Only keeping Kurtz alive, the Russian says he had nothing to do with these killings.

A group of men carrying Kurtz on a stretcher, appears from around the house. Waist deep in the grass, they appear to rise from

the ground. Naked human beings with spears, bows, and shields follow. The bushes shake and the grass sways, but then stop in "attentive immobility," as if everything waits for something to happen next. The Russian tells Marlow that if Kurtz does not say the right thing, they are done for.

Kurtz sits up. Marlow resents the absurd danger. Through his glasses, he sees Kurtz move his arm, talk, and nod his head. He realizes Kurtz means "short" in German, and feels the name fits, though he looks "at least seven feet long." The cage of his ribs and bones of his arms show. He thinks of Kurtz as an "animated image of death." Marlow hears Kurtz's deep voice from afar.

Kurtz falls back, then the savages carry him forward again. Some savages vanish into the forest, which after breathing them out, was drawing them back in.

Some pilgrims carry Kurtz's guns as they walk behind the stretcher. Bent over and talking, the manager walks beside him. They take Kurtz aboard the steamer and put him in a little cabin. Kurtz plays with the letters they had brought him. Marlow notices both the fire in Kurtz's eyes and the dullness. Speaking for the first time, he says to Marlow, "I am glad." Kurtz had received special recommendations about Marlow. The grave voice contains power. The manager appears in the doorway and the Russian stares at the shore. Marlow follows his glance.

A woman appears along the shore. She wears brass leggings to the knee, brass wire gauntlets to the elbow, and necklaces of glass beads. A "wild and gorgeous apparition of a woman," she walks with measured steps. She wears the "value of several elephant tusks upon her." The land, wilderness, and mysterious life seem to look at her. She approaches the steamer. Standing still, she faces them. The Russian growls, and the pilgrims murmur at Marlow's back. She lifts up her arms, the shadows darting out. Silence hangs over the scene. She turns and walks away, looking back at the men once.

The Russian says he would have shot her if she had tried to come aboard. He had been keeping her away from Kurtz for two weeks. According to the Russian, she had created problems. Once, while pointing at the Russian, she had to talk to Kurtz for an hour. Kurtz had been ill that day, or else "there would have been mischief." Marlow hears Kurtz yelling at the manager. He accuses him

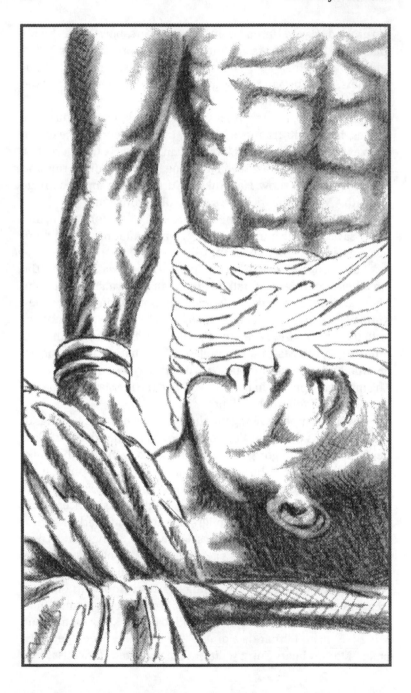

of caring only for the ivory. He says he is not as sick as the manager believes he is. The manager has interfered with his plans, and he will return to complete them. The manager walks from behind the curtain and tells Marlow how "low" Kurtz is, how he has done more harm than good for the company, and how they have done all they can for him. He agrees there is much ivory, but on the whole "the trade will suffer." Despite Kurtz's amazing success in obtaining ivory, the manager considers his method "unsound." Marlow ignores the manager's disapproval. He tells him that Kurtz is a remarkable man. The manager says Kurtz "was" a remarkable man. According to the manager, Marlow belongs to the same group as Kurtz.

Kurtz is "as good as buried," Marlow believes. The Russian taps Marlow on the shoulder and stammers out broken sentences. Marlow implores the Russian to speak. The Russian believes the white men hold ill-will toward him. Marlow agrees, saying the manager wants him hanged. The Russian plans to leave the area for a military post three hundred miles away. He asks Marlow to keep secrets so as to save Kurtz's reputation. Marlow promises.

He tells Marlow that Kurtz had ordered the attack to prevent them from taking him away. He is a simple man, though, and does not understand these matters. He has a canoe and three black fellows waiting for him. He asks for cartridges. Marlow hands them to him. The Russian takes some of Marlow's good English tobacco. He asks Marlow for shoes, showing him soles tied like sandals under his bare feet. Marlow gives him an old pair. He tells Marlow how Kurtz had read his own poetry, and he will never again meet a man like him. He rolls his eyes with delight and repeats how Kurtz had enlarged his mind. With cartridges in one pocket and the seamanship book in the other, the Russian vanishes. Marlow compares him to a "phenomenon!"

Marlow wakes after midnight. A fire burns on the hill, a line of agents guards the ivory, and men chant to themselves. Where Kurtz's "adorers" keep a vigil, red gleams waver in the forest against the intense blackness. Marlow dozes off again. When he wakes, he looks into the cabin and sees a light, but not Kurtz. An agent sleeps on a deck chair three feet from Marlow. Leaping ashore, Marlow says he will never betray Kurtz. He feels "jealous of sharing with any one the peculiar blackness of that experience."

Marlow discovers a trail in the wet grass. Kurtz crawls on all-fours. Marlow surprises himself by thinking of one of the knitting women. He believes he will never make it back to the steamer, instead living alone in the woods to an old age. He confuses the beat of the drums with that of his heart. He overcomes Kurtz, some thirty feet from a fire. Kurtz stands "like a vapor exhaled by the earth." He fears Kurtz will shout. A sorcerer, or witch-man, stands close behind them. Kurtz tells Marlow, "Go away—hide yourself." When Marlow asks Kurtz if he knows what he is doing, he says, "Perfectly."

Marlow threatens to smash Kurtz's head, even though nothing is near to use. Kurtz says his plans have been thwarted and he "was on the threshold of great things." Marlow assures him of success in Europe. He believes Kurtz belongs to no one, "nobody either above or below." His common words suggest dreams and nightmares. Kurtz's "perfectly clear" intelligence appears before Marlow. He says Kurtz's mad soul defies description. Marlow carries him back to the couch, comparing Kurtz's weight to a child's. He shakes, though, as if he "had carried half a ton on my back down that hill."

At noon the next day, with Kurtz aboard, Marlow steers the steamer away. Covered in dirt from head to foot, three men strut on the slope. Blacks fill the clearing, the black woman among them. They nod their horned heads, sway their bodies, and shake black feathers toward the river. The black woman puts out her hands and shouts. In chorus, the mob responds to her sounds, reminiscent of a "satanic litany."

In the pilot-house, Marlow asks Kurtz if he understands their actions. Kurtz answers, "Do I not?" Pulling the string of the whistle, Marlow scares the natives away. The pilgrims get their rifles. Someone on deck tells him to stop. The three men fall face down on the shore. Only the black woman remains in view. She stretches her arms after them over the river. The men aboard the boat begin firing, the smoke blocking Marlow's vision.

The steamer heads toward the sea at twice the speed it had come up the river. The manager watches Kurtz and Marlow. Kurtz is dying. The pilgrims look at Marlow with disfavor. He considers himself numbered with the dead. He accepts this "unforeseen partnership."

Kurtz mutters of his Intended, station, career, and ideas. He speaks of wanting kings to meet him at railway stations, a childish concept to Marlow. He insists on having the "right motives." He asks Marlow to close the shutters, and Marlow obliges.

The steamer breaks down, as Marlow had expected. One morning, Kurtz hands him papers and a photograph tied with a shoestring. He tells Marlow to keep them in his care, away from the manager, the "noxious fool." Kurtz mutters, "Live rightly, die, die...." Marlow believes he is rehearsing for some speech, or repeating a newspaper article.

Marlow spends more time helping the engine-driver fix the boat than speaking to Kurtz. One night, Kurtz says he is waiting for death. Marlow says, "Oh, nonsense." Marlow has never seen anything like the changes on Kurtz's face as he approached death. Kurtz's last words are, "The horror! The horror!"

Marlow goes to the mess-room and sits opposite the manager. He avoids his glance. Flies stream over the lamp, cloth, hands, and faces. The manager's boy peeks in the doorway, and says, "Mistah Kurtz—he dead." The pilgrims run to see, but Marlow stays to eat dinner. The voice is gone. The next day they bury Kurtz in a muddy hole. "And then they very nearly buried me," Marlow adds.

Marlow cannot compare himself to Kurtz, he says, because Kurtz had something to say. "The horror" is an expression of belief, a "moral victory paid for by innumerable defeats," he reasons. Kurtz had been able to summarize and judge with his final pronouncement. He remains loyal to Kurtz because of this conviction. Marlow returns to Europe, back to the "sepulchral city." He resents the sight of people hurrying about, drinking beer, and eating. He feels they do not know what he now knows. He often runs a fever and "was not very well at the time." His aunt tries to nurse him. He hears of Kurtz's mother's death, watched over by his Intended.

One day a company official stops by to get Kurtz's writings. Marlow says he had two fights about them with the manager, and he still refuses to give them up. The man says the company needs the reports, adding how it would be a great loss if he could not get the papers. Marlow finally gives him the "Suppression of Savage Customs" with the postscript torn off. He wants more. "Expect nothing else," Marlow says.

Two days later, another man, calling himself Kurtz's "cousin," appears. He is an organist and tells Marlow that Kurtz had been a talented musician. Marlow does not doubt this man's opinion. Marlow adds how to this day he does not know what Kurtz's profession was. He had been a painter, a journalist, a "universal genius." Marlow gives him some family letters and unimportant memoranda.

Then a journalist shows up. He considers Kurtz to have been a politician, an extremist leader. He says Kurtz could not write, but "heavens! how that man could talk." The man says Kurtz's faith could make himself believe anything. Marlow hands him the report, the man saying he will publish it. Left with a packet of letters and a portrait of a beautiful girl, he wants to visit Kurtz's Intended.

Kurtz's soul, body, station, plans, ivory, and career had passed out of Marlow's hands by now. Only his memory and this woman survive. He recalls one day when Kurtz had complained how the company would try to claim the ivory as theirs, though he had collected it himself. At her house, Marlow has a vision of Kurtz on a stretcher, as he whispers again "The horror! The horror!"

All in black, she comes forward in her drawing room. It is more than a year after Kurtz's death. She mourns for him, as if he had died "only yesterday." Marlow hands her the packet. When she asks Marlow if he had known Kurtz well, he says, "I knew him as well as it is possible for one man to know another." She had not been able to share her memories of Kurtz with anyone since his mother's death. Marlow says he had heard how her family had disapproved of the engagement.

They promise always to remember him. She says he will live on because of his words and because "his goodness shone in every act." She puts out her arms across the light of the window. This action reminds Marlow of the black woman's movements in the jungle. She regrets not being with Kurtz at his death. Marlow says he had stayed with him until the end.

When she asks about Kurtz's last words, Marlow says they were her name. She sighs, saying, "I knew it—I was sure!" Marlow believes he could not have told the truth, something too painful for her to bear. She hides her face in her hands and weeps. Marlow expects the house to collapse for telling a lie, but "the heavens do not fall for such a trifle."

We return to the *Nellie*, with Marlow in the pose of a meditating Buddha. The story is over. The Director says they have lost the first of the ebb. The narrator raises his head and sees a black bank of clouds, the tranquil Thames, and an overcast sky. All "lead into the heart of an immense darkness." The novella ends as it had begun, in darkness.

Analysis

Section III opens with the Russian extolling his admiration for Kurtz, his idol. "Something like admiration—like envy" for the Russian, Marlow listens to Kurtz's exploits—how he talks eloquently, discovers ivory and land, and receives adoration from natives.

The Russian never says anything derogatory or negative about Kurtz, even though Kurtz had tried to kill him over some ivory.

While Marlow by this time admires Kurtz, he rejects the Russian's complete devotion. Since the Russian "had not meditated over it," Marlow figures it to border on a "most dangerous thing."

The Russian embraces Kurtz "with a sort of eager fatalism." Marlow still judges him objectively. Considering Kurtz "mad," Marlow contrasts the Russian's unwavering idolization. This insight into Kurtz's behavior tempers Marlow's growing reverence. We also discover how Kurtz has suffered two illnesses, the nature of which we are not told.

By the next scene, however, when Marlow sees the heads attached to poles, we know that Kurtz suffers from mental illness. Marlow considers them "not ornamental but symbolic." "Food for thought," they show Kurtz's extreme policies. His actions exceed acceptable behavior. They show no "restraint in the gratification of his lusts." Not coincidentally, only one head faces Marlow, the rest pointing the other way. As a symbol, this represents Kurtz staring at Marlow, or Marlow coming to terms with his other half, the side similar to Kurtz, where desires dominate logic.

Marlow attributes Kurtz's madness to the jungle. By taking a "terrible vengeance" out on him, it has forced Kurtz to abandon morality and reasonable judgment. The whispering forest echoes "loudly within" Kurtz because he is "hollow at the core...." This shatters Marlow's earlier image of Kurtz.

At this point, Marlow compares Kurtz's world to a "region of subtle horrors." He denounces Kurtz, considering him "no idol of mine." The Russian opposes Marlow's refutation by justifying Kurtz's savagery. Since the heads belonged to rebels, Kurtz had no choice. Marlow rejects the Russian's explanation. A few moments later, Kurtz appears for the first time. Marlow sees him "in the gloom," while he stands "in the sunshine." This contrast of light and dark shows how Marlow still isolates himself from Kurtz's world. The natives trail behind, though, as if they follow a god.

When Marlow notices Kurtz's deep voice, he completes the idea he had established earlier—Kurtz as more of a spiritual being than a physical one. Kurtz's "thin arm," "bony head," and eyes of an "apparition" de-emphasize his physicality. Marlow thinks of him as "an animated image of death carved out of old ivory."

On the boat, Kurtz's first words to Marlow, "I am glad," represent an ironic acknowledgment. Since people had mentioned Marlow to Kurtz, they show the simple pleasure of meeting someone. However, we know Marlow feels the same way toward Kurtz, even with his recent doubtings. Marlow could have spoken these words, in turn.

Kurtz's black mistress, "the wild and gorgeous apparition of a woman," links him to a woman in Africa the way his Intended connects him to a woman in Europe. Although the pilgrims and the Russian disapprove of her, she stands immune from their censure. She is a reverse Kurtz in a female form, though more of a physical presence with her "flash of barbarous ornaments." She never speaks, whereas Kurtz is a voice. Her "savage and superb" physical strength opposes Kurtz's physical frailty.

The manager questions Kurtz's sanity by calling his methods "unsound." He believes he lacks judgment. Marlow defends Kurtz, saying, "Nevertheless, I think Mr. Kurtz is a remarkable man." Marlow sides with Kurtz for two reasons. First, he dislikes the manager, so this contradiction, he knows, annoys him. Second, when he finds himself "lumped along with Kurtz," he takes it as a compliment.

This affinity determines the next scene, when Marlow promises the Russian that he will save Kurtz's reputation by keeping his savagery secret. Marlow surprises himself. "I did not know how truly

I spoke," he says. When the Russian flees the area, we see a further connection with Marlow. The Russian has a "canoe and three black fellows waiting" to take him away. This parallels Marlow's steamer and crew on a smaller level. The Russian also needs shoes, which Marlow gives him. Remember earlier, Marlow needed shoes when the helmsman's blood had soaked into them. The Russian also says he will never meet such a man again. We know Marlow feels the same way.

The next scene turns dream-like. Marlow falls asleep, then awakes after midnight with fires burning and drums filling the air "with muffled shocks and a lingering vibration." The natives keep "their uneasy vigil" over Kurtz's house, a religious connotation. When Marlow chases Kurtz through the jungle to get him back to the boat, we notice how possessive of him he feels. He says he is "jealous of sharing with any one the peculiar blackness of that experience." Yet, he shares the memory of Kurtz with us as he narrates his adventure.

Kurtz's crawling on all-fours to escape links him to the native in Section I who had crawled on all-fours to drink from the river. They both crawl to survive, they both are near death, and they both fall victim to the jungle. And, since the natives worship Kurtz, they should share similarities.

In the fragmented conversation with Kurtz, Marlow fluctuates between wanting to kill Kurtz and assuring him of success in Europe based on his accomplishments. Marlow knows that Kurtz personifies contradictions. There is nothing "above or below him"; he is mad, yet intelligent; and, he is "alone in the wilderness," yet Marlow "supported him, his long bony arm clasped round my neck." During the next scene, the natives and black mistress line the jungle to watch Kurtz leave, their god being taken from them. She leads them in a "roaring chorus," suggesting a religious response at a formal service. When Marlow asks Kurtz if he understands their actions, he smiles and says, "Do I not?" He understands their devotion, and how removing him betrays their belief.

Marlow then scares the natives, to the dismay of some people on the boat. He fears for his life, so he blows the whistle. Only the black mistress remains, her arms "stretched tragically" in the pose of a priestess. She stays devoted until the end, the same way Kurtz's Intended, another woman, will at the end.

As they escape "out of the heart of darkness," Marlow contin- ues his dedication to Kurtz. The manager and pilgrims look upon him with "disfavor." His "unforeseen partnership" with Kurtz forges his complicity. Marlow even helps Kurtz by closing the shutters to the outside, as he requests. Kurtz's separation from the jungle un- nerves him. He does not want to leave Africa and his followers the same way Marlow does not want to leave Kurtz. This explains why Marlow murmurs "Oh, nonsense" when Kurtz says he waits for death. "The horror! The horror!"—Kurtz's last words—suggest many interpretations. They refer to his death, his destroyed plans, his sub- mission to his evil side, and the pain of life. Marlow "blew the candle out" and then left the cabin. This extinguished light signifies not only Kurtz's life, but the sanctity he embodies for Marlow.

Appropriately, a native announces Kurtz's death. Marlow would not because he would rather deny it. Since Kurtz represents a god, his followers should pronounce his death. Ironically, Marlow ap- pears "brutally callous" by not remaining with Kurtz, we know, this is not true. His emotional closeness to Kurtz surpasses any pilgrim's. Marlow agrees with the Russian when he proclaims Kurtz's great- ness. Kurtz "had something to say." His judgment, as summarized in "The Horror!" expresses conviction and an "appalling face of a glimpsed truth." Kurtz's life extended to extremes. He "stepped over the edge," while Marlow "had been permitted to draw back his hesitating foot." Marlow withdraws where Kurtz advances.

This distinction represents the Freudian psychological terms ego and id. The id is man's instinctual impulses and the satisfac- tion of primal needs. This is Kurtz, the man who satisfies his needs by returning to the primitive forest. He lets loose his urges, no matter how excessive or deviant they are. Conversely, Marlow is the ego—the part of the personality that controls behavior and ex- ternal reality. He questions the savagery, killing, and abandonment of laws for pleasure.

Marlow never relinquishes his rational side for Kurtz's irratio- nal one. Marlow is the way Kurtz once was, and Kurtz is what Marlow does not want to be. When Marlow returns to Europe, the daily routine of working, eating, and drinking bores him. His ex- perience has taught him things these people can never know. He feels like "laughing in their faces so full of stupid importance."

He runs a fever, fulfilling the doctor's predictions in Section I, when he had said that the changes take place inside. Like Kurtz, Marlow is mentally, not physically, ill. His "inexcusable behavior" proves the jungle's influence.

The visits by the company official, Kurtz's "cousin," and the journalist illustrate their impersonal concern for Kurtz's life, unlike Marlow's deeply personal one. They want his papers for official and public reasons. Marlow gives them only unimportant papers, saving the personal letters and photographs for Kurtz's Intended. Marlow finds the seamanship book and Kurtz's writings. He gives the book to the Russian because he knows he values it, and Kurtz's letters to his Intended because she values them.

Marlow's last act—his visit to Kurtz's Intended more than a year after his death—completes Marlow's journey. She constitutes the European version of Kurtz's black mistress in Africa. Her "fair hair," "pale visage," and "pure brow" oppose the black woman's ornamental excesses. She speaks of her loss to Marlow. The black woman had expressed it through physical movements. They talk of intimacy, knowing Kurtz, and love. Ironically, she says she "knew him best." In many ways, Marlow knows Kurtz on a deeper level than she does. She also is unaware of his black mistress, barbaric actions, and mental illness. She says he "drew men towards him." For Marlow, nothing could be more true. Mesmerized by Kurtz, he remains loyal to his memory. Marlow avoids breaking the "illusion that shone with an unearthly glow" in Kurtz's Intended. He believes she is not capable of dealing with the truth, a force too powerful to oppose. Her misconception shows when she says Kurtz's "goodness shone in every act." Marlow agrees, furthering the deception. He connects Kurtz's Intended to the black mistress. These women show their love for Kurtz by cherishing their image of him—each mirroring their culture's ways.

Let's return for a moment to the oil painting Marlow had seen in Section I. We now recognize a reference to the black mistress and his Intended in the picture. The blindfold and torch reflect his Intended, her delusion toward Kurtz and her light of love in his dark world. The somber, black background and stately movement reflect his black mistress, the African jungle and her measured gestures. With only Kurtz's words left to them, Marlow and the

woman talk of his verbal gifts. When she wants to know Kurtz's last words, Marlow lies and tells her they had been her name, not "The horror! The horror!"

Earlier, in Section I, Kurtz had said he detested a lie because there is a "taint of death" in it. He lies to Kurtz's Intended to shield her from the truth. He has seen the truth in the jungle, but knows the lie here is better. Kurtz's Intended cries, and, in so doing, comforts herself. It would have been "too dark altogether" for her. Marlow finalizes his idea of "how out of touch with truth women are," which he had announced in Section II. He also atones, in a way, for his attitude toward his aunt for helping him secure his job. There he had belittled a woman, here he protects a woman.

The framed narrative ends. We return to the *Nellie* and Marlow's "pose of a meditating Buddha." As we had asked in Section I, what has he learned and suffered? Now we can answer these questions. He has learned of man's darker side, his attraction toward evil, through Kurtz. He has discovered how the heart of darkness is not only a physical place (Africa), but a place within all men. He has suffered from seeing that darker side. Few people can claim this, which explains why Marlow "sat apart," from the others on the boat. Finally, the Director says, "We have lost the first of the ebb." He ignores Marlow's tale. Nothing reaches him, none of the philosophy and insights into human nature. The narrator lifts his head and sees "the heart of an immense darkness" in the distance. Marlow's story has enlightened him. If we have listened, it has done the same for us.

Study Questions

1. Why does the Russian nurse Kurtz through two illnesses?

2. What frightening sight does Marlow see outside Kurtz's house?

3. Who is with Kurtz when Marlow first sees him?

4. Why does the manager disapprove of Kurtz?

5. Why does the Russian leave Kurtz's area?

6. Why is Kurtz carried from the forest?

7. Why does Kurtz give Marlow papers before he dies?

8. Explain the irony of where they bury Kurtz.

9. Why do three people visit Marlow when he returns to Europe?

10. What lie does Marlow tell Kurtz's Intended?

Answers

1. The Russian's admiration and love for Kurtz compels him to nurse Kurtz through two illnesses.

2. Marlow sees heads stuck on poles outside Kurtz's house.

3. Weak, Kurtz is on a stretcher carried by the natives when Marlow first sees him.

4. The manager disapproves of Kurtz because he believes Kurtz has done more harm than good for the company by his unsound methods.

5. The Russian leaves Kurtz's area because he fears the manager wants him killed.

6. Kurtz is taken from the forest to a cabin on the boat so he can be rescued and cured.

7. Kurtz gives Marlow a packet of letters to preserve his work and memory.

8. Worshipped in life by the natives, Kurtz is buried in a "muddy hole," a place of filth and emptiness.

9. Three people visit Marlow in Europe to get Kurtz's writings.

10. He tells her Kurtz's last words were her name.

Suggested Essay Topics

1. From what the Russian says, he worships Kurtz. He always praises him, even justifying Kurtz's barbaric killings. Marlow admires Kurtz also. How, though, does their admiration for Kurtz differ? Is the Russian's more exaggerated, and Marlow's more controlled? Since the Russian already knows Kurtz and

has spoken to him, and Marlow has not met Kurtz yet, can that influence their respective feelings?

2. There are many indications of Kurtz's mental illness. The decapitated heads on poles outside his home, his "exterminate all the brutes" philosophy, and his obsessive quest for ivory show his "unsound method," as the manager terms it. Is Kurtz mad, or has he simply adapted to a barbaric society? Is he just playing by the rules of the jungle, which differ from those of a civilized society?

3. Though seemingly minor, the three women are important to Marlow's adventure. His aunt, Kurtz's black mistress, and Kurtz's Intended influence the story in various ways. Compare the three of them. What does each one represent? Include how they come from different parts of society with separate values and beliefs, especially Kurtz's two loves.

4. Kurtz appears in *Heart of Darkness* for a very short time. He does and says little. Why then is he so important to the story? Why didn't Conrad expand his actual role? Does his limited appearance detract from his importance?

5. Describe the three people who visit Marlow to get Kurtz's papers after he returns to Europe from Africa. What do their positions and interest in Kurtz say about Kurtz's reputation? Why is Marlow so reluctant about giving them Kurtz's papers? What are his personal reasons for protecting them?

6. Besides Marlow and Kurtz, Conrad identifies all the characters who appear by description, not name. We see the chief accountant, the manager, the manager's uncle, the helmsman, the Russian, etc. Why does Conrad use these vague references? By not giving them names, does he shift the emphasis away from them, even though they all contribute to Marlow's journey? Is their function, as suggested through their title, more important than their name?

Sample Analytical Paper Topics

Topic #1

Marlow's conflicting feelings toward Kurtz depend on a number of things. Sometimes he admires him, other times he denounces him. Write an essay analyzing these opposing feelings.

Outline

I. Thesis Statement: *Based on Kurtz's actions and ideas, Marlow's feelings toward him alternate between admiration and reprehension.*

II. Feelings of admiration

    A. Kurtz's talents

        1. Obtained ivory.

        2. Organized the natives to work for him.

        3. Wrote of his experience and honestly evaluated them.

    B. Idolatry for Kurtz

        1. Natives performed sacrifices in his honor.

        2. The Russian worships him.

        3. Marlow honors Kurtz's memory to protect him.

III. Feelings of reprehension

    A. Kurtz abandoned morality

        1.   Killed people who opposed him (heads on poles).

        2.   Threatened to kill the Russian over ivory.

   B.   Kurtz shows little restraint

        1.   Covets ivory and its importance.

        2.   Regards the natives as inferior people. "Exterminate all the brutes" he wrote in his report.

        3.   His methods are "unsound."

IV.   Conclusion: Depending on what aspect of Kurtz Marlow considers, his feelings vary from one extreme to the opposite, from respect to revulsion.

Topic #2

Who is the main character in *Heart of Darkness*, Marlow or Kurtz? Develop an argument showing how each one can be viewed as the main character.

Outline

I.   Thesis Statement: *Marlow and Kurtz each can be considered the main character. One cannot exist without the other.*

II.   Kurtz is the main character

   A.   He is Marlow's goal

        1.   Marlow becomes obsessed with meeting Kurtz along the journey.

        2.   Kurtz represents a side of Marlow that he is afraid to become.

   B.   All the people and action revolve around Kurtz

        1.   The chief accountant, manager, and other company workers deal with Kurtz.

        2.   All the ivory trading goes back to Kurtz.

III.   Marlow is the main character

   A.   As narrator, Marlow's story is more important

   1. Marlow's feelings and judgment govern what the reader knows.

   2. The story shows his change after the journey.

   3. Marlow is in the entire novella, Kurtz isn't.

B. Marlow makes Kurtz a great figure

   1. Only Marlow admires Kurtz in an extreme way.

   2. After Kurtz's death, Marlow keeps him alive by preserving his memory.

IV. Conclusion: An argument can be made for either Marlow or Kurtz as the main character.

Topic #3

Heart of Darkness shows how the forces of nature control man. The jungle exposes man's weakness. Write an essay showing how nature dominates all the people in the jungle.

Outline

I. Thesis Statement: *The jungle influences everyone's behavior. It not only affects them physically, but also mentally. It exposes man's weakness in many ways.*

II. Nature's power

A. The forest's trees and heat

   1. Makes it difficult for the boats to sail.

   2. Blocks the natives and seamen from each other.

B. Affects men physically and mentally

   1. Causes the helmsman's death.

   2. Marlow's fever.

   3. Kurtz's insanity.

III. Man's weakness

A. Man must adapt to survive

   1. Lack of food and water affects their behavior.

2.   Breakdown leads to violence.

IV.   Conclusion: Nature's power overwhelms man, exposing many weaknesses. Either mentally or physically, all the characters in *Heart of Darkness* succumb to nature's force.

Topic #4

The title *Heart of Darkness* refers to Africa as well as a psychological side of man. Develop these two meanings of the title.

Outline

I.   Thesis Statement: Heart of Darkness *is both a metaphor for an internal side of man, and a literal allusion to Africa. It simultaneously suggests a physical and mental reference.*

II.   It is a literal place

   A.   Africa is the dark continent

      1.   Savages live there.

      2.   Dense jungle shades the land.

      3.   It is separated from the civilized world.

   B.   Inequalities of power

      1.   Whites control the natives.

      2.   Abuse of power for ivory and wealth.

      3.   Marlow despises the whites and empathizes with the natives.

III.   It is a psychological reference

   A.   Suggests man's dark side

      1.   Kurtz's irrational acts.

      2.   Marlow's illness after meeting Kurtz in Africa.

      3.   Natives' extreme devotion to Kurtz, a mad god.

IV.   Conclusion: *Heart of Darkness* refers to both physical and mental aspects of the novella. These external and internal worlds influence each other.

Topic #5

Women play a prominent role in Marlow's experience in Africa. Without them, his story is incomplete.

Outline

I.   Thesis Statement: *Though in the background, the three women who appear in* Heart of Darkness *play an important role in Marlow's journey to and from Africa.*

II. Marlow's aunt

    A. She is the only "family" Marlow mentions

    B. She helps him secure his position in the company

    C. He visits her before he leaves for Africa

    D. She refers to him as an "emissary of light"

    E. She nurses him through his illness when he returns

III. Kurtz's black mistress

    A. She is Kurtz's love in the jungle

    B. Marlow admires her physical beauty

    C. She never speaks, unlike Kurtz, who Marlow says is a "voice"

    D. She follows Kurtz when they take him to the boat

    E. The pilgrims shoot her as they leave

IV. Kurtz's Intended

    A. She contrasts Kurtz's black mistress

        1. She lives in Europe

        2. She talks

        3. She shows her emotions

    B. Marlow visits her after meeting Kurtz

        1. Marlow gives her Kurtz's important papers

        2. Marlow lies to protect her from the truth

V.   Conclusion: In a predominantly male world, Marlow's aunt, Kurtz's black mistress, and Kurtz's Intended affect him before, during, and after his experience in Africa.

Topic #6

The three sections in *Heart of Darkness* serve as borders around Marlow's journey from London to Africa and back.

Outline

I.   Thesis Statement: *Though Conrad uses a non-chronological narration, he separates* Heart of Darkness *into three sections to show Marlow's emotional and literal progression as he journeys to Africa to meet Kurtz.*

II. Section I establishes Marlow's introduction to Kurtz

   A.   Marlow joins the company and undergoes a physical

   B.   He works his way from the Outer to the Inner Station

   C.   He hears about Kurtz for the first time from the manager and accountant

III. Section II develops Marlow's interest in meeting Kurtz

   A.   Marlow thinks of his journey in terms of speaking to Kurtz

   B.   He gets closer to Kurtz's station

   C.   The natives attack Marlow's boat from their proximity

   D.   Marlow meets the Russian at Kurtz's station

IV. Section III culminates in Marlow finally meeting Kurtz

   A.   The Russian speaks of Kurtz's greatness

   B.   Marlow meets Kurtz and speaks with him privately

   C.   Marlow shares in Kurtz's death

   D.   Marlow preserves Kurtz's memory when he meets Kurtz's Intended

V.   Conclusion: Each section of *Heart of Darkness* establishes a deeper relationship between Marlow and Kurtz.

Topic #7

Conrad incorporates many symbols. As with most symbols, their meanings vary with different interpretations or approaches.

Outline

I.   Thesis Statement: *Through the use and frequency of symbols in* Heart of Darkness, *Conrad deepens the meaning of the story. Taken separately or in pairs, they add another level of analysis beneath the surface narrative.*

II. Objects as symbols

    A. Kurtz's painting of the blindfolded woman

    B. Heads on poles outside of Kurtz's hut

    C. Shoes

        1. Marlow's shoes.

        2. The Russian's shoes.

    D. Books.

        1. *An inquiry into Points of Seamanship.*

        2. Kurtz's writings.

III. Animals (non-humans) as symbols

    A. Black hens at Fresleven's death

    B. Snake in reference to the river on the map

    C. Hippos/hippo meat

    D. Flies over the dying agent, then over Kurtz

IV. Places as symbols

    A. Europe

    B. Africa

    C. Thames River

    D. Jungle River

V.   Conclusion: Conrad's symbols embody more meanings other than their actual reference. By interpreting them in different ways, we expand the profundity of *Heart of Darkness*.

SECTION SIX

Bibliography

Conrad, Joseph. *Heart of Darkness and The Secret Sharer*. New York: Bantam Books, 1981.

Conrad, Joseph. *The Nigger of the Narcissus*. New York: Dell Publishing Company, Incorporated, 1960.

Gurko, Leo. *Joseph Conrad: Giant in Exile*. New York: The Macmillan Company, 1962.

Karl, Frederick R., and Magalaner, Marvin. *A Reader's Guide to Twentieth-Century English Novels*, New York: Octagon Books, 1984.

Available at your local bookstore or order directly from us by sending in coupon below.

Available at your local bookstore or order directly from us by sending in coupon below.

MAXnotes®

REA's Literature Study Guides

MAXnotes® are student-friendly. They offer a fresh look at masterpieces of literature, presented in a lively and interesting fashion. **MAXnotes®** offer the essentials of what you should know about the work, including outlines, explanations and discussions of the plot, character lists, analyses, and historical context. **MAXnotes®** are designed to help you think independently about literary works by raising various issues and thought-provoking ideas and questions. Written by literary experts who currently teach the subject, **MAXnotes®** enhance your understanding and enjoyment of the work.

Available **MAXnotes®** include the following:

Absalom, Absalom!	Henry IV, Part I	Othello
The Aeneid of Virgil	Henry V	Paradise
Animal Farm	The House on Mango Street	Paradise Lost
Antony and Cleopatra	Huckleberry Finn	A Passage to India
As I Lay Dying	I Know Why the Caged	Plato's Republic
As You Like It	Bird Sings	Portrait of a Lady
The Autobiography of	The Iliad	A Portrait of the Artist
Malcolm X	Invisible Man	as a Young Man
The Awakening	Jane Eyre	Pride and Prejudice
Beloved	Jazz	A Raisin in the Sun
Beowulf	The Joy Luck Club	Richard II
Billy Budd	Jude the Obscure	Romeo and Juliet
The Bluest Eye, A Novel	Julius Caesar	The Scarlet Letter
Brave New World	King Lear	Sir Gawain and the
The Canterbury Tales	Leaves of Grass	Green Knight
The Catcher in the Rye	Les Misérables	Slaughterhouse-Five
The Color Purple	Lord of the Flies	Song of Solomon
The Crucible	Macbeth	The Sound and the Fury
Death in Venice	The Merchant of Venice	The Stranger
Death of a Salesman	Metamorphoses of Ovid	Sula
The Divine Comedy I: Inferno	Metamorphosis	The Sun Also Rises
Dubliners	Middlemarch	A Tale of Two Cities
The Edible Woman	A Midsummer Night's Dream	The Taming of the Shrew
Emma	Moby-Dick	Tar Baby
Euripides' Medea & Electra	Moll Flanders	The Tempest
Frankenstein	Mrs. Dalloway	Tess of the D'Urbervilles
Gone with the Wind	Much Ado About Nothing	Their Eyes Were Watching God
The Grapes of Wrath	Mules and Men	Things Fall Apart
Great Expectations	My Antonia	To Kill a Mockingbird
The Great Gatsby	Native Son	To the Lighthouse
Gulliver's Travels	1984	Twelfth Night
Handmaid's Tale	The Odyssey	Uncle Tom's Cabin
Hamlet	Oedipus Trilogy	Waiting for Godot
Hard Times	Of Mice and Men	Wuthering Heights
Heart of Darkness	On the Road	Guide to Literary Terms

RESEARCH & EDUCATION ASSOCIATION
61 Ethel Road W. • Piscataway, New Jersey 08854
Phone: (732) 819-8880   **website: www.rea.com**

Please send me more information about MAXnotes®.

Name _____

Address _____

City _____ State _____ Zip _____